ADMONITIONS

FOR

SUNDAY-SCHOOLS;

WRITTEN FOR A PARTICULAR PARISH

AND NOW PUBLISHED

FOR GENERAL USE.

BY A LAYMAN.

A NEW EDITION.

LONDON:

Printed for J. WALTER, CHARING CROSS;
And F. and C. RIVINGTON, St. Paul's Church-Yard,
Bookfellers to the Society for promoting Chriftian Knowledge.

M DCC XCIX.

ADVERTISEMENT.

THE Author hopes he shall not be thought to intrude in the clerical office, by the following publication. His view was, to furnish the children of the Sunday-school, in the parish where he resides, with a few plain, practical lessons, for them to read over in a winter's evening: but by no means to divert their attention from the better instructions they receive from the pulpit. And, though this work was designed principally for one parish, he flatters himself that, if approved, it may be of equal use in others.

CONTENTS.

A 2   ADMO-

ADMONITION,

ADMONITION I.

3d Epiſtle of St. JOHN, 4th verſe.

I have no greater joy than to hear that my children walk in truth.

BY " Truth" is here meant the word of God: and to " walk in truth" ſignifies to live according to that word ; to make the holy ſcripture the rule of our lives and actions. So to "walk with God," is the ſame as to obey God, or to keep his commandments : — to " walk uprightly," is to live honeſtly :—to " walk in love," is to live in brotherly love one with another, and to do all the good we can by acts of love and kindneſs :—to walk in Chriſt," or " in the light," is to follow Chriſt, or to govern our lives and conduct by the light of his goſpel ; to imitate his example, and to obey his laws. And ſurely there can be no greater joy to parents, and to all who have the care of children, than to ſee them (as the text expreſſes it) " *walk* " *in truth*"—to find that the pains beſtowed upon them have not been beſtowed in vain ; but that they have made a right uſe of the inſtructions they have received, by leading virtuous and good lives. This, my dear children, is the end and deſign of our taking you into this

ſchool;

school; to train you up in the way of godliness, which is the way of happiness; trusting in the blessing of God on our endeavours, that you may walk therein all the days of your life, and that as you grow in *age* you may "*grow in* "*grace.*"— Our first object was, to prevent your *doing evil*; our next is, to teach you to do well. Ignorance and idleness are the never-failing sources of wickedness and misery. Ignorance of religion, and of our duty, is the worst sort of ignorance: and idleness on the Lord's day is the worst sort of idleness. The design of setting up these schools was to prevent or remove those dreadful evils, by instructing you in religious knowledge, and by keeping you well employed on the day set apart for religious exercises. We saw, with great concern, a number of children in this parish, loitering about on Sundays, instead of going to church, and doing their duty;— some playing—others talking idly, or worse than idly. We now see them decent and orderly: reading their bibles, and other good books; and attending at church regularly twice a day. Those who once knew nothing of God and their duty, now know both, by being instructed in the holy scriptures, which alone will "make them wise unto salvation." What an happy change! How pleasing must it be to your parents! and how peculiarly so to us your instructors, to see you thus walk in the knowledge and practice of religious truth. But remember that this is only the beginning of a good work. You are now but just setting out in the way wherein you should go. It is a good thing to *begin* well: but

but the great matter is, to *go on* so ;—to continue improving in knowledge and goodness ;—to be diligent and constant in the performance of your several duties ;—not only to spend the *Sabbath* day well, but to spend *every* day well;—to pray to God every day of your lives for his help and protection, and to thank him most humbly and heartily for his blessings already vouchsafed to you ;—to be always well employed ; — to make yourselves as useful as you can to your parents, and all your other relations and friends ;—and to shew your gratitude to us, by making a good use of the benefits you have received from us in this place of religious instruction. This is the return we expect and desire, for the time, and money, and labour, we have bestowed upon you ; and great will be our joy and comfort if we receive it. We are pleased indeed with thinking that we have done *our* duty; by putting you in the way of doing *your's* : but it will be a sad disappointment and grief to us, if you fail on your part, and we find that we have been labouring in vain. Our aim is to make you happy : your endeavour must be to make yourselves so ; as you certainly may, if you will. Consider often and seriously the great advantages you enjoy, and remember what our blessed Saviour declares, that "to whom much is given, of them shall much be required." The more has been done for you, the more you must do for yourselves : the more good seed has been sown in your hearts, the more good fruit you must bring forth in your lives and conversations. And

great

great will be your reward, both in this life and
the next, for so doing: in this world, you will
have peace of mind and a good conscience, the
best of all earthly blessings; and in the world to
come, joy and happiness for ever and ever.——
To help you forward in the way of salvation
(besides our constant prayers to God, and the
regular instructions in the school), I have drawn
up some short and easy lessons, in the form of
Admonitions, for your reading at home; and that
they may answer the good end proposed by
them, I must beg you to look them over very
carefully, and think of them often. And above
all, I charge you to pray earnestly to Almighty
God, that he will give you understanding to
know, and grace to perform, your duty; that
he will keep you stedfast and unmoveable in the
truth of the gospel; that so both you and we
may REJOICE EVERMORE IN THE LORD.

ADMONITION II.

PROVERBS iii. 17.

Her ways are ways of pleasantness.

WHOSE ways? you will naturally ask:
for you must certainly desire to find
them out: and when you have found them,
to walk in those ways all the days of your life.
Consult your bible, and there you will find the
true answer—Solomon will shew you this most
" excellent way."

In the 13th verse of the chapter from which
my text is taken, you will read these words:
" Happy

" Happy is the man that findeth WISDOM, and the man that getteth UNDERSTANDING." Now if you want to know what is meant by wifdom and underftanding, look again into your bible, Job xxviii. 28. and there you will find, that " the fear of the Lord, *that* is wifdom; and to depart from evil, is underftanding:" fo that wifdom, in fcripture language, fignifies religion, or godlinefs. And of *this* it is that Solomon fpeaks, when he fays, " Her ways are ways of pleafantnefs"—and, " all the things thou canft defire are not to be compared unto her." St. Paul in like manner affures us, that " godlinefs is profitable unto *all things :*" that is, it has *every* real advantage attending it; " having the promife of the life that *now is,*" as well as " of that which *is to come.*" Now one of the good things of this life is pleafure : it is what we all defire and feek after ; but what many mifs of, becaufe they look for it where it is not to be found. It is indeed to be found only in the way of godlinefs, or in a life of religion and virtue. This the fcripture declares in the plaineft manner, and this I hope to convince you of in the following difcourfe. I will fhew you, firft, that religion gives us the greateft of all pleafures, which nothing elfe can give; and, fecondly, that it heightens every other pleafure : fo that its ways may moft properly and truly be called the WAYS OF PLEASANTNESS.

There is an old faying, and a very true one, that " a good confcience is a continual feaft." The meaning of it is, that a fenfe or confcioufnefs of doing our duty, or of leading a good and

religious

religious life, gives conſtant pleaſure to the
mind, which is the greateſt of all feaſts. Food
to the *body* is pleaſant; but that is a ſhort pleaſure, and to be had only for a few minutes in
the day. But food to the *mind* is laſting: a
good conſcience is a *continual* pleaſure; that
never ceaſes, and never cloys. The mind is
always at work, and giving us either pleaſure or
pain, according as we do well or ill. Conſcience
is a voice within us, that will be heard, whether
we will or no. It will accuſe us, and give us
bitter pain and uneaſineſs, when we neglect or
tranſgreſs our duty; and it will commend us,
and give us great pleaſure and comfort, when
we do right. We may fly from other people;
but we cannot fly from ourſelves; we cannot
fly from our own hearts; nor from God, who is
every where preſent, who ſearcheth our hearts,
who knoweth all our moſt ſecret thoughts and
deſigns, as well as our outward actions. It is
he that pours joy and comfort into the heart
that is pure and holy, and bitter ſorrow and
anguiſh into that which is impure and ſinful:
" For if our heart condemn us, God is greater
than our heart, and knoweth all things. Beloved, if our heart condemn us not, then have
we confidence towards God." Take notice of
theſe words,—" then have we confidence towards God:" that is, if our hearts aſſure us that
we do our duty, and live as we ought to do,
then we may be aſſured of God's love and favour—we may draw near to him in prayer with
humble confidence;—we may be certain of
being rewarded by him both in this world and
the

the next. And, let me afk you, Is not this
pleafure? is it not the greateft of all pleafures,
to feel our minds eafy and happy, and to know
that we are in favour with God, who is the
author and giver of all goodnefs! And it is a
pleafure we may all have, if we will;—high
and low, rich and poor, all are alike capable of
being good, and confequently of being happy.
—Next to the pleafure of a good confcience,
and being in favour with God, is that of being
in favour with worthy and good men: and this
pleafure you are fure to have by the fame means;
that is, by leading a religious and virtuous
life.—Another pleafure that I think you muft
feel is, that of making a proper return to us,
who have taken pains to bring you into thefe
good ways. You muft furely be pleafed by
giving us pleafure; which you may all do by
behaving as you ought, and continuing fteady
in the performance of your duty. We can have
no greater joy than to fee and hear of our children " walking in truth."

I might mention other pleafures in life, of a
leffer fort and value; all which (fuch, I mean,
as are innocent) religion allows and approves
of; and which without religion are indeed of
no value, and can give us no true comfort and
fatisfaction. A diftempered mind, like a diftempered body, makes us incapable of every
enjoyment. What pleafure can the beft food
give to a fick ftomach? What joy can a perfon in pain receive from the moft agreeable di-
verfion? Much lefs can an uneafy mind (as
every bad perfon's is) feel any pleafure or com-

A 6 fort

fort from any, or all, of what are called the pleafures of life. But a good confcience gives a relifh to every good thing befides :—it enlivens every amufement ;—it caufes a cheerful countenance as well as a merry heart.

I fhall only make one obfervation at prefent upon what has been difcourfed to you, which I wifh to imprefs deeply on your minds. How good and kind is God, to make our duty and pleafure thus go hand in hand! fo that by following the one we are fure to obtain the other. To make the fame road the " way of pleafantnefs" in *this* life, and the way that leads to thofe " pleafures which are at his right hand for evermore" in the life to come.

ADMONITION III.

PROV. iii. 17.

Her ways are ways of pleafantnefs.

WHAT ftrange and falfe notions do fome people entertain of religion !—as if it was a dull and melancholy thing; an enemy to all pleafure and cheerfulnefs: whereas it is in truth the great friend and promoter of both. Its " ways are ways of pleafantnefs," fays Solomon: and the Pfalmift tells us, that " the voice of joy and gladnefs is in the dwellings of the righteous"—that " the ftatutes of the Lord rejoice the heart"—that God's " law is his delight." So again in the New Teftament ;—" His commandments are not grievous"—" The fruit of the Spirit is joy"—" Rejoice in

6

the

the Lord always," fays St. Paul; " and again I fay, Rejoice"—And in another place, " Rejoice evermore."

In my laft difcourfe I fhewed you the pleafures of religion in general. We will now confider the feveral branches of it in particular; as it is divided into our duty towards God, our neighbour, and ourfelves; and we fhall find, that its ways are, in every one of thefe, " ways of pleafantnefs;" and that a good life is, in every refpeft, a joyful and an happy one.

To begin with our duty towards God.— Now if we truly and fincerely believe in God; if we think of him as we ought; if we look up to him as our Maker, Preferver, and Redeemer; as the Author and Giver of all good things; as our heavenly Father, in whom " we live, move, and have our being;" as " the Father of our Lord Jefus Chrift, the Father of mercies, and the God of all comfort:" what pleafure, what joy, muft we feel in fuch thoughts and reflections!—Again: if we love him with all our hearts, and put our whole truft in him; if we exprefs our love, and truft, and thankfulnefs to him, in prayer and praife; if we worfhip him, and give him thanks, both in private and public: what delight and comfort muft we receive from thus difcharging our duty towards him! How pleafantly, as well as profitably, is our time thus employed! On the Lord's day more particularly, what an honour and pleafure is it to enter his courts, and join our prayers and thankfgivings in the congregation of the faithful! " I was glad," fays David, " when they

said

said unto me, Let us go into the house of the Lord:"—And surely every sincere Christian must say and think the same; and " call the Sabbath a delight,"—a day of true pleasure, as well as of religious exercise and improvement. —The last, but most material, part of our duty towards God is, " to serve him truly all the days of our life." And what a pleasure must it be to serve so good and gracious a Master! to think that he will kindly accept our poor and imperfect services; and to be assured, that he will reward them with peace of mind in this world, and with joy and happiness unspeakable in that which is to come.

Next to the love of God comes the love of our neighbour; which includes our whole duty towards him: for so we are told by St. Paul, that " he that loveth another hath fulfilled the law;" and that " it is briefly comprehended in this saying, Thou shalt love thy neighbour as thyself." The meaning is, that love, if hearty and sincere, will shew itself in our lives and actions, and put us upon doing every kind and good office in our power; upon discharging all the relative and social duties of life. It will make us good parents and children, good neighbours, and good friends. It will keep us continually well employed, and endeavouring to make one another happy. And is not this, think you, the way of pleasantness? a way that you would all wish to walk in? And let me tell you, for your comfort, that it is a way open to every body:—old and young, rich and poor, all may do their duty, all may be useful in life, all may
do

do *fome* good; and therefore all may be happy. Other pleafures are fhort and uncertain; hard to come at, and often attended with pain and difappointment; but the pleafure of doing good is fure and lafting; eafy to be procured, and will never difappoint us. To inftruct the ignorant, to affift the helplefs, to comfort the afflicted, to encourage one another to love and to good works; thefe are duties we may all perform, thefe are pleafures we may all partake of.

Laftly, the duties that more immediately refpect ourfelves; fuch as, fobernefs, temperance, and chaftity; diligence and induftry. Thefe are all productive of pleafure and comfort. To be fober, temperate, and chafte, is the only way to be healthy; and health gives pleafure. To be active and induftrious, while it makes the body ftrong and vigorous, makes the mind cheerful and pleafant. The food we eat has a double relifh, if earned by our own labour, and " the fleep of the labouring man is fweet." Even our play and diverfions require induftry in working to make us enjoy them; I mean when they are ufed as a relief from toil and bufinefs, and not made our chief bufinefs and employment. In fhort, there is no way of paffing our lives comfortably, of enjoying health of body and peace of mind, but by " doing our duty in that ftate of life to which it has pleafed God to call us." You, my good children, have a great advantage in being thus early brought into the ways of religion and virtue; in being fo foon taught your duty, and fo frequently and earneftly exhorted to practife it. You are but juft entering into life:

you

you have much time before you: make the most of it: and if you continue, as you have begun, in the right way, happy will it be for you both in this world and the next. The farther you advance in the knowledge and practice of your duty, the more pleasant and delightful you will find it. Remember you have a good and gracious God, whose laws are not grievous; and a merciful Saviour, whose " yoke is easy," and whose " burden is light:" who will safely guide all his faithful servants through this life; and will at last bring them to mansions of eternal joy and happiness in the life to come.——— God grant we may all thus live and die in the Lord!

ADMONITION IV.

Eccles. xii. 1.

Remember now thy Creator in the days of thy youth, while the evil days come not, nor the years draw nigh, when thou shalt say, I have no pleasure in them.

To " remember our Creator," signifies, to think of him; to meditate on his glorious nature and perfections; to consider him as always present with us, and as the constant witness of all our thoughts, words, and actions. Thus Moses says, in his exhortation to the Israelites, Deut. viii. 18. " Thou shalt *remember* the Lord thy God." And the pious Psalmist, to the same purpose, declares, " I have set the Lord always before me." And again: " I will
remember

remember the works of the Lord." And in another pfalm: " I have *remembered* thy name, O Lord; and HAVE KEPT THY LAW." Which laft expreffion leads me to obferve, that to remember God, in the text and elfewhere, fignifies, not barely to think of him, but to remember him *practically*; that is, fo to think of him as to ferve and obey him: For " the mercy of the Lord" (as David fays in the ciiid Pfalm) " is upon them that fear him; to fuch as keep his covenant, and to thofe that REMEMBER HIS COMMANDMENTS TO DO THEM."

But to proceed with my text. You are told to remember God NOW; for the *prefent* is the only time you are fure of: " Now is the accepted time, NOW is the day of falvation." You are therefore to remember him " *now*, in the days of your youth:" for *now* you are moft able to do it; *now*, in the time of your health and vigour, will your fervices be moft acceptable to God; *now* will they be the fureft evidence of your love and reverence towards him, and of your fincere and hearty defire to pleafe him; *now*, too, they will be moft ufeful and profitable to yourfelves. By an early piety and obedience, you will make the difcharge of your duty eafy and familiar to you, and lay a fure foundation of future comfort and happinefs. By fetting out at firft " in the way wherein you fhould go," you will be better able, and difpofed, by God's grace, to continue in it all the days of your life; and as you advance in years, to increafe in virtue and godlinefs. You will find the ways of wifdom, or religion, to be

" ways

" ways of pleasantnefs," as well as of peace. By a grateful remembrance of the Author and Giver of all good things, you will have a double enjoyment of the bleffings of life : and by a firm truft in his mercy and goodnefs, you will bear the evils of it with patience and refignation; " knowing that all things work together for good to them that love and obey him."—Thefe are the great advantages of remembering and ferving God in your youth; "while the evil days come not, nor the years draw nigh, when thou fhalt fay, I have no pleafure in them :"— that is, before the approach of old age; which is in itfelf evil and burdenfome, but becomes far more grievous and terrible when loaded with the remembrance of paft fins, and embittered with the dreadful profpect of death and judgment to come—when many pains and infirmities will naturally attend us, and when there can be no pleafure or comfort but in a good confcience and the recollection of a well-fpent life. They who have been forgetful of God, and negligent of their duty, in their younger days (fuppofing they fhould live to be old, and have a due fenfe of their wickednefs), will at beft pafs the decline of life in continual fhame and forrow. But fhould they be cut off in the midft of their evil courfes, or live till they are hardened in fin, think only how dreadful muft be the confequence. In the grave there is no room for repentance or amendment: they that die in their fins will infallibly rife to condemnation and eternal mifery. And as to a death-bed repentance, befides the extreme folly and pre-
fumption

fumption of trufting to what may never happen,
I fee no good grounds in fcripture for fuppofing
it will be accepted, fo as to be available to falvation. The gracious promifes of the gofpel are
made to thofe that lead good and holy lives, not
to dying penitents. It is " by patient conti-
nuance in well doing" (that is, by a conftant
and perfevering courfe of good actions and good
living), that we are taught to feek for, and affured that we fhall obtain, " eternal life." Now
the fooner we enter on fuch a courfe, the eafier
we fhall find it, and the greater progrefs we fhall
make in it. On our firft fetting out in life,
much, if not every thing, depends. Habits early
contracted, whether good or bad, generally accompany us through life. Befides, we are told,
that God will " reward every man according to
his deeds." The fooner therefore we begin to
work in his fervice, the greater will be our reward in heaven. Let us then lofe no time;
when, if well employed, it will turn to fo good
account. You, my good children, have been
early trained up in the knowledge of God and
of your duty. Be it your care and ftudy to
make the beft ufe of thefe great privileges and
benefits. Let the remembrance of your Creator be ever in your minds; let the fear and love
of him be deep'y impreffed in your hearts; and
let it be your earneft and conftant endeavour to
ferve and pleafe him all the days of your life.
" Worfhip the Lord with holy worfhip,"—pray
to him daily for his grace and protection; praife
him daily for his goodnefs and mercies. Remember that God is gracious, and will not forget

get your works done in obedience to his commands. "Be ye," therefore, "ftedfaft, unmoveable, always abounding in the work of the
Lord; forafmuch as ye know that your labour
is not in vain in the Lord."

ADMONITION V.

1 THESS. v. 17.

Pray without ceafing.

WE have many exhortations to this purpofe
in St. Paul's epiftles—to "*continue in*
prayer"—to "*continue inftant* in prayer"—
"praying *always* with all prayer and fupplication
in the fpirit"—"in *every* thing by prayer and
fupplication, with thankfgiving, to let our re-
quefts be made known unto God:"—and our
bleffed Saviour, we are told, "fpake a parable"
unto his difciples, "to this end, that men ought
always to pray, and not to faint." But we are
not to fuppofe, by any of thefe expreffions, that
either Chrift, or his apoftle, meant that we fhould
be *always* actually employed in prayer; nor
even that the *greateft part* of our time fhould be
devoted to it. For this would be inconfiftent
with the common bufinefs and duties of life;
which our holy religion requires us to attend to
carefully, and to difcharge with diligence and
induftry. What is the true meaning and intent
of thefe, and the like, precepts, and particularly
of that in the text, I fhall endeavour to fhew you
in the following difcourfe.

Now to "pray without ceafing," I apprehend,
implies

implies thefe three things. Firft, that we fhould be regular and conftant in our times and feafons of praying: fecondly, that we fhould be earneft, and in fome degree importunate, in it: and, laftly, that we fhould be always in a fit habit and difpofition for it.—Order and regularity are neceffary upon all occafions. No bufinefs can be done well, no duty can be properly performed, without them. And fo it is in regard to prayer. If we have not ftated and regular times for praying, we fhall neglect, or forget it; and at laft perhaps entirely lay it afide. " Evening, and morning, and at noon, will I pray," fays the pious pfalmift. And of Daniel, it is recorded, that he prayed conftantly " three times a day." Twice a day, my good children, you fhould never fail offering up your prayers to God: in the morning, to thank him for preferving you through the night paft, and to beg his bleffing for the enfuing day; and in the evening to blefs him for the mercies of the day, and to implore his protection for the following night. But on every Sunday, or Lord's day, a much larger portion of your time fhould be employed in prayer and devotion. The Almighty has gracioufly allowed you fix days out of feven to work, and provide for the good things of this life. The feventh day he has confecrated for his worfhip and fervice. Remember that it is your bounden duty, as well as your intereft, to fet it apart for that purpofe. Never fail, I charge you, to go to church twice a day: and always bear in mind the *end* of your going thither; namely, to worfhip God, and to be inftructed in your duty.

You

You should also spend some part of the day in reading good books at home, and thinking of what you have heard at church. A Sunday well employed will most likely ensure you an happy week.—Another particular implied in the text is, that we should be earnest, and in some sort importunate, in our prayers. Not that you should aim at any high flights or raptures of devotion (which is too often the case with hypocrites, and bad people) but the meaning is, that you should keep your minds *intent* on what you are about; that you should pray with your *hearts*, as well as with your lips. And if you are thus attentive and sincere, you will naturally feel some degree of warmth and earnestness in your addresses to the throne of grace. At least, you will not " faint,' as our Saviour expresses it ; that is, you will not be cold and indifferent in your prayers. But, on the other hand, I must caution you against one fault, which is very common among children, and among some grown people; and that is, against speaking with too loud a voice when you say your prayers. For this answers no good purpose. It rather hinders, than promotes, your own devotion; and it disturbs that of others. Observe, I beg of you, the excellent direction given you in your common prayer book, to accompany the minister with "an *humble*," or *low* "voice," in such parts of the service as you are to repeat after him: and the same rule I would advise you to follow when you pray in private.

Lastly; tho' we are not required to be always praying, yet we are required to be always in a

fit

fit habit and difpofition for it. By which I mean, that we fhould endeavour to preferve a devout frame and temper of mind, and to live under a continual fenfe of God's infinite power and goodnefs, and of our intire dependence on him, and obligations to him. Without fuch a difpofition, our prayers are mere empty words; a mockery of God, inftead of an acceptable fervice to him. Above all, we muft be careful to lead an holy and virtuous life, remembering what the wife man tells us, that " the facrifice of the *wicked* is an abomination to the Lord: but the prayer of the *upright* is his delight." And to the fame purpofe we read in the New Teftament, that " God heareth not finners: but if any man be a worfhipper of God, and doth his will, HIM HE HEARETH."

ADMONITION VI.

COLOSS. iii. 15. --latter part.

And be ye thankful.

THERE is no furer fign of a good and well-difpofed heart than thankfulnefs, or gratitude. On the other hand, nothing fhews a bafe and depraved one more than the want of thankfulnefs, or ingratitude. It was a common faying among the Romans, and a very true one, " Call a man ungrateful, and you call him every thing that is bad." And one of the wifeft writers among them obferves, that " there is no bad quality but what dwells in the breaft of the ungrateful." In fcripture we find ingratitude
make

make a part of the very worſt of characters.
Thus St. Paul, ſpeaking of the ancient heathen
world, ſays, that "when they knew God, they
glorified him not as God, *neither were thankful*."
And in another epiſtle, foretelling the exceeding
great wickedneſs of " the laſt days," among
other inſtances of it, he ſays, that " men ſhall be
unthankful."

As Almighty God is the author and giver
of all good things, of all that we enjoy here, or
hope for hereafter ; ſo he is, or ought to be, the
firſt object of our gratitude. " Unto THEE, O
GOD, do we give thanks : yea, unto THEE do
we give thanks." To him it is, that we are
commanded in the text to " be thankful:" and
to him we are directed, throughout the bible,
to offer up our tribute of praiſe and thankſgiving. " Be ye thankful," is the voice of nature,
and the voice of God. The book of Pſalms is
one continued leſſon, as well as example, of this
duty. The pious effuſions of a grateful heart
ſhine there in the moſt ſublime and animated
language. From thence we may learn that
thankſgiving is a moſt material and eſſential
part of devotion ; and that, in all our addreſſes
to the throne of grace, we ſhould add praiſe to
prayer. So we read of Daniel, a bright pattern
of piety and holineſs, that "he kneeled upon his
knees three times a day, and prayed, and *gave
thanks* before his God, as he did aforetime ;"
that is, as it had been his conſtant practice. So
again, we read in the Acts of the Apoſtles, that
the firſt Chriſtians not only " continued ſted-
faſtly in the apoſtles' doctrine, and in prayers ;"
but

but that they were " daily with one accord in the temple, and breaking bread from house to house, *praising God.*" If we look into the epistles of St. Paul, we shall find him, like David, full of gratitude and thankfgiving; and continually exhorting others to follow his example. Thus he charges the Ephefians to be " giving thanks always for all things unto God and the Father, in the name of our Lord Jefus Chrift." And to the Theffalonians he fays, " In every thing give thanks; for this is the will of God in Chrift Jefus concerning you." And again to the Hebrews, " By him therefore let us offer the facrifice of praife to God continually." For the due performance of this duty, I can give no inftructions fo good as what you may meet with in your common-prayer book. Look into that admirable form, called " the general thankf- giving," and there you will find for what, and in what manner, you are to thank " the father of all mercies." You are to thank him, moft humbly and heartily, for all his goodnefs and loving kindnefs, both to you and to all men ; for your " creation, prefervation, and all the bleffings of this life," all which proceed from his bounty and goodnefs. But "above all" you are to thank him for his amazing and " inef- timable love in the redemption of the world by our Lord Jefus Chrift," the foundation of our pardon and falvation; " for the means of grace" here, and " for the hope of glory " hereafter, procured us by his merits and medi- ation. And, fince we can difcharge no part of our duty, nor confequently pay our debt of

B   gratitude

gratitude to God, as we ought, without the
affiftance of his Holy Spirit ; you muft therefore
befeech him to give you "fuch a due fenfe of
all his mercies, that your hearts may be un-
feignedly thankful; and that you may fhew
forth his praife, not only with your lips, but in
your lives." Hence you are to learn, that
without a fincere and thankful heart, and a good
and holy life, all our praifes and thankfgivings
are of no value in the fight of God; they are
mere empty words; nay worfe, they are vile
hypocrify. And becaufe it is only a fteady,
conftant, uniform, and lafting obedience, that
can fhew the fincerity of our thankfulnefs, or
make our praifes acceptable unto God; you
muft pray that, by the help of his grace, you
may "give up yourfelves" *intirely* "to his fervice, and walk before him in holinefs and righteoufnefs *all your days.*" If therefore you would
fulfil the precept in the text, let a grateful fenfe
of God's love and kindnefs dwell in your hearts
continually. Let your lips fpeak the language
of your hearts. And, above all, let your lives
be anfwerable to both. Let them be one continued facrifice of praife and thankfgiving to
him, in whom you "live, move, and have your
being."

You muft alfo remember to be thankful to
man, as well as to God; firft to your parents,
whofe love and care of you, you fhould endeavour to repay, as well as you can, by every act
of dutiful attention ; helping and fupporting
thofe in their old age, who have nurfed and
taken care of you in your infancy and youth.

2   You

You should be thankful likewise to your friends and benefactors; particularly to those who have watched over you in your tender years, and instructed you in the most useful of all knowledge, that of the holy scriptures; "which alone can make you wise unto salvation, thro' faith in Christ Jesus." All the return we desire is, that you will make a good use of our instructions. We have trained you up "in the way wherein you should go." Be it your care, by the grace of God, "never to depart from it."

ADMONITION VII.

Luke xi. 2.

When ye pray, say, Our Father, which art in Heaven.

My design from these words, is not to explain to you the Lord's prayer; that is so well done already in the catechism, and the book of sections, that I think it needless to add any thing upon the subject. But what I mean is, to shew you *what it is* to pray, and *how* to pray as you ought: and this with a particular view to the Lord's prayer, as being the best of all prayers, and what we are taught constantly to use, whenever we address God, either in private or public. You may think perhaps that to *pray*, and to *say your prayers*, is one and the same thing; and that if you say them every morning and evening at home, and on Sundays when you go to church, you have done all that is required of you. But this, my dear children, is a great mistake; for to *pray*, is an act of the mind or heart,

D 2

and

and may be done without opening our lips. On the other hand, barely to *say* one's prayers, is the work of the mouth; and if it does not come from the heart, is of no fort of ufe whatever, nor can it properly be called *praying*. Inftead of doing our duty to God in this refpect, it is an affront and infult offered him, if we pray with our lips, and not with our hearts. They fhould indeed both go together; and when we lift up our minds to heaven, it is natural, and it is right, that we fhould exprefs our thoughts and defires in fuitable words. For fo our Saviour directs us — " WHEN YE PRAY, SAY, ' and then follows that excellent form of words, which he has gracioufly taught us, wherein to offer up our devotions properly and acceptably, at all times and on all occafions. But how fhould this prayer be faid? Surely with more than ordinary care and deliberation. Whereas the way in which it is commonly repeated, is, I am forry to obferve, more hafty, and carelefs, and flovenly, than that of faying any other prayer whatever; without fo much as the *appearance* of devotion, or even of attention. It is more like the chattering of parrots, than like a religious act of a rational creature. I do not fpeak of you children in particular; but of the too general way of faying the Lord's prayer by people of every age, both in church and out. It is hurried over fhamefully, as if it were a thing of courfe, a matter of mere form, not worth attending to. And I am fure it never *can* be attended to in that manner of faying it. It certainly is not *praying*: it is rather a falfe fhow, or an abufe of prayer, a moving of the lips, without any motion of the heart.

heart. It is no better than a mockery of God, to whom the prayer is addreſſed; and an inſult on our Saviour, who taught us the uſe of it. And can you expect to be heard, or that your petitions will be granted, when offered up in ſo negligent and thoughtleſs a way? " Be not deceived: God is not to be mocked." He has a right to our utmoſt reverence and reſpect: to the ſervice of our hearts and ſouls; to our warmeſt love and adoration. He will not be put off with *lip-ſervice*, or with vain pretences of praying. Let me only aſk you one queſtion. Suppoſing you had a favour to beg of any of *us*; would you ſpeak to us in that haſty, careleſs way, in which you ſay the Lord's prayer? Would not you rather ſpeak ſlowly, handſomely, and reſpectfully? You *ought* ſo to do, and you certainly *would* do ſo, if you expected to have your requeſts granted. And would you treat God Almighty with leſs reſpect than you do one of your fellow creatures? Conſider, I intreat you, when you ſay the Lord's prayer, or any other, who it is you are ſpeaking to. It is to your great Creator, the Lord of heaven and earth, in whom you " live, move, and have your being:" on whom you intirely depend for life, and ſupport, and every thing;—to the God who, " heareth prayer:" who hears, and regards the ſincere and devout petitions of his faithful ſervants; but no other. Conſider alſo the *ſubject* of your prayers. It is to pray to him for all you want; to thank him for all you have; to beg his bleſſing on you both in this life, and in that which is to come. For HIS " is the kingdom, and the power, and

the

the glory, for ever and ever." And if you thus
serioufly confider, *who* you are praying to, and
what you are praying for, you cannot furely be
at a lofs, *how* to pray. You muft fee the pro-
priety, and abfolute neceffity, of praying with
clofe attention and humble reverence and devotion; and of faying your prayers flowly, clearly,
and deliberately. Never mind what others do;
never follow bad examples. They will be no
excufe to you. By your *own* act, by your *own*
praying, you will ftand, or fall, in the fight of
God. It is not the length of a prayer, but the
devotion and fincerity of heart, with which it is
put up, that he regards. Better fay five words
with your underftanding and attention, than ten
thoufand without. Even a *filent* prayer from
the *heart* is better than the longeft or fineft com-
pofition, that proceeds only from the *mouth*.
The Lord's prayer itfelf is in fact no prayer to
him who ufes it improperly or indecently.

To conclude. What St. John fays of the
great duty of *love*, is equally applicable to that
of *prayer*. "My little children, let us not *pray*
in word, neither in tongue," *only*: "but in deed,
and in truth." And that we may fo pray, let
us remember at all times, and in all places, that
we are addreffing ourfelves to God, who is every
where prefent; on earth, as well as in heaven;
and who has declared, that "them that honour
him, he will honour; and that they that defpife
him, fhall be lightly efteemed." Let us therefore "give unto the Lord the glory due unto
his name: let us worfhip the Lord with holy
worfhip."

ADMONITION VIII.

Exodus xx. 8.

Remember the Sabbath-day, to keep it holy.

THE appointment of the fabbath is as old as the creation; or rather, it immediately followed it. For 'fo we read, in the 2d chapter of Genefis; that as foon as " the heavens and the earth were finifhed," God " bleffed the feventh day, and fanctified it." The word, "*fabbath*," you are to obferve, fignifies *reft*. And to " *fanctify*," or " *hallow*," is to make *holy*; or to devote any thing to an holy ufe or purpofe. So that the fabbath, you fee, is to be obferved both as a day of reft, and of worfhip. The very name implies the one; and the command, to keep it holy, exprefsly requires the other.—That we may obferve it as we ought, let us inquire what is to be *done*, and what is to be left *undone*, on that facred day.

In general, it is to be devoted to the fervice of Almighty God; to be employed in his worfhip, both in public and private. Our private devotions indeed fhould never be omitted on any day; our public ones are required only on Sunday. We fhould then go to church regularly twice a day; to pray to God, to praife and thank him for all his goodnefs; to hear his holy word; and to be inftructed in our duty. Befides this, we fhould fpend fome part of the day in ferious thought and meditation; in reading the bible, and other religious books. We fhould confider with ourfelves how we have employed

B 4

the

the week paſt; and if we recollect any faults we
have committed, repent, and reſolve to avoid
the like in future. We ſhould alſo take every
opportunity of inſtructing the ignorant, and thoſe
that are younger than ourſelves, in the principles and duties of religion. All offices of kindneſs and charity, ſuch as viſiting the ſick, reliev-
ing the needy, and comforting the afflicted, are
particularly ſeaſonable on the Lord's day. By
performing thoſe duties we may be ſaid, in a
double ſenſe, to keep it holy. But we muſt ab-
ſtain from all labour and working, (except works
of neceſſity and charity) in order to keep it as a
day of reſt: and from all play and diverſions, in
order to keep it as a day of holineſs. From ſin
and wickedneſs of all ſorts we are indeed to refrain *every* day alike. Yet ſurely on this ſacred
day ſin may be ſaid to be "exceeding" or *doubly*
"ſinful;" as it is a proſtitution of the ſabbath, as
well as an offence againſt the other laws of God.
Drunkenneſs, for inſtance, is at *all* times a vice
moſt ſhameful and abominable. On a *Sunday*
it has the guilt of profaneneſs added to it. A
Sunday ſpent idly, is generally ſpent wickedly.
If not kept *holy*, it is commonly made more
unholy than any other day of the week. And
the reaſon is plain. Idleneſs naturally leads to
vice and folly. He that is not well employed,
will be ill employed. When work is laid aſide,
and religious exerciſes neglected, time will not
barely be loſt, but abuſed: and the ſin of *omiſſion*
will be followed by ſins of *commiſſion*. Many
that have ended their lives at the gallows have
declared, that they began their wicked courſes
by

by spending the Lord's day idly and profanely. What was intended for their good, has become by their abuse of it, an occasion of their falling into sin and destruction.

How good and gracious is God in all his dispensations to man? His laws and commandments are not only " holy and just," but wisely and mercifully designed for our benefit and happiness. This, in particular, of observing the sabbath, is evidently calculated for the ease and relief both of man and beast; as well as for our improvement in religious knowledge and practice. It is, if rightly understood, a delightful, as well as a profitable institution. If our minds are well disposed, we shall take pleasure in every return of the Lord's day: we shall " enter into his courts with praise, and serve him with joy and gladness." We shall consider it as the beginning of a good week to us; as insuring God's blessing upon our labours and undertakings for the other six days. And we shall also look upon it (as we are directed to do in St. Paul's epistle to the Hebrews) as a pledge or earnest of our *future* " rest" in heaven; of that *eternal* sabbath, which " remaineth to the people of God."

" Remember" therefore " the sabbath-day, to keep it holy." When you have left this school, recollect often how you passed it during your attendance here, and let it be an example for you to follow ever after. Never fail going to church: not as a matter of custom, or form, or decency; but as it is your bounden duty, and your highest interest so to do. Go

B 5

thither

thither, not to look about you, or to talk with your neighbours; but to worſhip God. Look only at your books, converſe only with your Maker. Be clean and decent in your dreſs; but think no farther about it. A pure heart, an humble and devout ſpirit, is the only ornament that God requires, and delights in.—Many of you, I obſerve it with pleaſure, are fond of pſalm-ſinging, and ſing well. By all means let me encourage you in it. It is a delightful, it is an heavenly, entertainment; as well as a mate-rial part of public worſhip. It is good at *all* times: on *Sundays* it is peculiarly ſo. Idle tat-tling and goſſiping is always bad: on Sundays in particular. But in an hour or two's friendly converſation, after the duty of the day is over, there is no harm.—I ſhall conclude with my hearty prayers to God (in which I hope you will all join me) that he will diſpoſe you ſo to paſs this and every day of your lives, that you may "apply your hearts unto wiſdom."

ADMONITION IX.

Exodus xx. 13.

Thou ſhalt not kill.

OR, as we read in the prayer-book, "Thou ſhalt do no murder." A crime ſo heinous, ſo horrid, ſo truly diabolical, that nature ſhud-ders at the very thought of it. But beſides the actual commiſſion of murder, there are many ways by which you may be guilty, though in a leſſer degree, of the ſin here forbidden. With-

out

by spending the Lord's day idly and profanely.
What was intended for their good, has become
by their abuse of it, an occasion of their falling
into sin and destruction.

How good and gracious is God in all his dif-
pensations to man? His laws and commandments are not only " holy and just," but wisely
and mercifully designed for our benefit and
happiness. This, in particular, of observing the
sabbath, is evidently calculated for the ease and
relief both of man and beast; as well as for our
improvement in religious knowledge and practice. It is, if rightly understood, a delightful,
as well as a profitable institution. If our minds
are well disposed, we shall take pleasure in every return of the Lord's day: we shall " enter
into his courts with praise, and serve him with
joy and gladness." We shall consider it as the
beginning of a good week to us; as insuring
God's blessing upon our labours and undertakings for the other six days. And we shall also
look upon it (as we are directed to do in St.
Paul's epistle to the Hebrews) as a pledge or
earnest of our *future* " rest" in heaven; of that
eternal sabbath, which " remaineth to the people
of God."

" Remember" therefore " the sabbath-day,
to keep it holy." When you have left this
school, recollect often how you passed it during
your attendance here, and let it be an example for you to follow ever after. Never fail
going to church: not as a matter of custom, or
form, or decency; but as it is your bounden
duty, and your highest interest so to do. Go

B 5

thither

thither, not to look about you, or to talk with your neighbours; but to worfhip God. Look only at your books, converfe only with your Maker. Be clean and decent in your drefs; but think no farther about it. A pure heart, an humble and devout fpirit, is the only ornament that God requires, and delights in.—Many of you, I obferve it with pleafure, are fond of pfalm-finging, and fing well. By all means let me encourage you in it. It is a delightful, it is an heavenly, entertainment; as well as a material part of public worfhip. It is good at *all* times: on *Sundays* it is peculiarly fo. Idle tattling and goffiping is always bad: on Sundays in particular. But in an hour or two's friendly converfation, after the duty of the day is over, there is no harm.—I fhall conclude with my hearty prayers to God (in which I hope you will all join me) that he will difpofe you fo to pafs this and every day of your lives, that you may "apply your hearts unto wifdom."

ADMONITION IX.

EXODUS xx. 13.

Thou fhalt not kill.

OR, as we read in the prayer-book, "Thou fhalt do no murder." A crime fo heinous, fo horrid, fo truly diabolical, that nature fhudders at the very thought of it. But befides the actual commiffion of murder, there are many ways by which you may be guilty, though in a leffer degree, of the fin here forbidden. With-

out

out taking away a man's life, you may injure
him in his character; you may hurt his health;
you may deftroy his peace of mind; you may,
by your ill treatment of him, fhorten his days,
or make them uncomfortable. And every offence of this kind is in fact a breach of the fixth
commandment.

"Whofoever hateth his brother," fays St.
John, "is a murderer." As "*love* is the *fulfil-
ling* of the law," *hatred*, of courfe, muft be the
tranfgreffing of it; and particularly of this part
of the law which forbids murder. All fin takes
its rife from the heart: "Out of the heart," fays
our Saviour, "proceed MURDERS." So that
if you bear malice or hatred in your heart, you
are in the fcripture fenfe guilty of murder.
And it is plainly with a view to this commandment I am fpeaking of, that the catechifm tells
you, in the account of your duty towards your
neighbour, that you muft " bear no malice nor
hatred in your heart." But indeed hatred feldom ftops there; it generally proceeds to bad
words and bad actions, which are great aggra-
vations of the guilt of a bad heart. Accordingly,
the catechifm tells you, " to hurt nobody by
word or deed." But you may think, perhaps,
that mere words can hurt nobody; and that if
you refrain from injurious actions, you may give
a vent to your paffion in *faying* what you pleafe.
Look into the 5th chapter of St. Matthew, and
you will find a very different account of the m t-
ter. "Ye have heard," fays our Saviour, "that
it was faid by them of old time, Thou fhalt not
kill; and whofoever fhall kill, fhall be in dan-

ger

ger of the judgment:" that is, the Jews confidered only the ftrict letter of the law, and taught that actual murder would expofe a man to punifhment. "But I fay unto you," fays Chrift, "that whofoever is angry with his brother without a caufe, fhall be in danger of the judgment: but whofoever fhall fay, Thou fool, fhall be in danger of hell-fire:" A plain proof, that by words, as well as actions, we may break the commandment, and be punifhed for it everlaftingly. God fearcheth our hearts; and "there is not a word in our tongues, but thou, O Lord, knoweft it altogether," and wilt moft affuredly call us to account for it at the day of judgment.

There is one way in which the fixth commandment is too often broken, which you may little think of, but which deferves your moft ferious confideration; I mean, by the bad behaviour of undutiful children towards their parents. This is fometimes, in the ftrict and literal fenfe, committing murder. How many, alas! have by this means had their lives fhortened, as well as made miferable. To take away the life of thofe who, under God, gave us life, is furely a fin of the deepeft dye; the moft horrid fpecies of murder. And believe me, every wicked and undutiful child is in fome degree guilty of it. To break a parent's heart, is not only killing, but torturing; and in any way to give forrow or uneafinefs to thofe, whom it fhould be our ftudy to make eafy and happy, is a double offence againft God; as being a breach both of the fifth and fixth commandment.

To

To conclude: Every wicked perfon, of whatever age or ftation he may be, is in fome fort a murderer; as he difturbs the peace of fociety, and leads others into fin. In this refpect he is truly a follower of the devil, who is faid to have been " a murderer from the beginning;" inafmuch as he brought fin and death into the world, and ftill continues to deftroy the fouls of men by his temptations.—But "be ye followers of God, as dear children:" keeping his commandments, and walking in love; after the example of your bleffed Mafter, who came into the world, "not to deftroy men's lives, but to fave them."

ADMONITION X.

Exodus xx. 15.

Thou fhalt not fteal.

BESIDES the groffer acts of theft or robbery, there are many leffer forts of the fame fin forbidden by this commandment: fuch as, fraud, or cheating, of every kind; neglecting to pay debts; taking advantage of other men's neceffities; impofing on their ignorance in matters of trade, or bargains; unfaithfulnefs to one's truft; and, in fhort, whatever is contrary to ftrict honefty and juftice, and to that excellent rule of doing as one would be done by. And here it is neceffary to caution young people in particular againft the firft beginnings of this fin: againft doing wrong in fmaller matters; againft pilfering, or cheating, in things of

little

little value; left (as is generally the cafe) they go on from bad to worfe, and become at laft hardened in wickednefs. For in this, as in all other fins, few people begin with the higheft crimes, and few ftop at the loweft. One naturally leads to another, and fo draws them on by degrees to death and deftruction. Bad habits are feldom, if ever, got rid of; and none perhaps grows upon a man more than that of thieving, or difhonefty. He foon lofes his character; nobody will truft or employ him; he knows not how to get a livelihood by fair means, and fo has recourfe to the worft; and moft likely ends a miferable life in prifon, or at the gallows. Or fhould he efcape punifhment in this world, (which is very feldom the cafe), he is fure to meet with it, in everlafting mifery, in the world to come: for we are exprefsly told, that "thieves "fhall not inherit the kingdom of God;" and that "the Lord is the avenger of all fuch as go beyond and defraud their brother *in any matter.*" Obferve thefe laft words; which fhew that God will feverely punifh not only the notorious thief and robber, but whofoever is guilty of any fraud, or over-reaching, even in leffer inftances; " in any," and every, " matter," without exception. "Ye fhall not fteal, neither deal falfely, neither lie one to another. Thou fhalt not defraud thy neighbour, neither rob him." Levit. xix. 11—13. Remember alfo what our bleffed Saviour fays: " He that is faithful in that which is leaft, is faithful alfo in much; and he that is unjuft in the leaft, is unjuft alfo in much." Luke xvi. 10. Accuftom
yourfelves

yourselves therefore to be strictly honest and
just, and faithful to your trust, in the most trifling concerns, and things of the smallest consequence, that you may learn to be so in matters
of greater importance: and be careful to avoid
every act of thieving, or cheating, in the least
instances, lest you get into bad habits, and commit greater crimes. Be assured, that for every
transgression of your duty you must be accountable to God. If you steal or cheat never so
secretly, you cannot escape his notice and his punishment. He will not admit of any excuses for
fraud or dishonesty. You must not think to
plead poverty, or hunger, or distress of any kind.
Work for your livelihood, and honest industry
will never fail to procure it. To eat the bread of
idleness is bad, even when no dishonest means
are used to obtain it; but when idleness and
thieving go together (as it commonly happens) the sin is doubled, and great indeed is
the guilt of the sinner. But you may think perhaps, that if you take from another a small pit-
tance of what he has in great abundance, you do
him no injury, and therefore there is no harm in
it. Be not deceived: the sin is the same in *you*,
though the consequence of it may not be so bad
to *him*. Servants, in particular, are apt to take
very improper liberties with what belongs to
their masters or mistresses, under a false notion
that they have a right to partake of it; or (what
is still worse) give away a portion of it to others,
because they would be kind and generous. But
this again is a *double* crime: it is adding breach
of trust to dishonesty. To give away what is
not

not your own to difpofe of, is not charity, but
cheating, or rather downright injuftice.

Borrowing, and not paying, is another way of
breaking the commandment, too commonly
practifed by perfons of every age and condition;
but not the lefs finful for being common. In
this cafe, the borrower receives no lafting
benefit; and the lender is hurt, and often
ruined, by it. It is beft, therefore, not to bor-
row at all. You will thereby keep clear of one
fort of difhonefty, and prevent much mifchief
and diftrefs both to yourfelf and others.

I cannot conclude this fubject better, than
by advifing and exhorting you moft earneftly, in
the words of the catechifm, " not to covet, nor
defire, other men's goods; but to learn and labour truly to get your own living; and to do
your duty in that ftate of life unto which it fhall
pleafe God to call you." Honefty is the beft
policy: and " HE THAT WALKETH UPRIGHTLY
WALKETH SURELY."

ADMONITION XI.
MATTHEW vii. 21.

*Not every one that faith unto me, Lord, Lord,
fhall enter into the kingdom of heaven: but he
that doeth the will of my Father which is in
heaven.*

THIS declaration of our bleffed Lord to
his difciples, is one of thofe many paf-
fages of fcripture, which fhew the neceffity of
obedience

obedience to the will of God, in order to our salvation, or to our being admitted into the kingdom of heaven. They are so plain, that one would think it impossible to mistake their meaning; or unnecessary to do any thing more than barely to repeat them. For as the gospel was to be "preached to the *poor,*" so the most important parts of it are level to the lowest capacity. He that *runneth* may read, and he that readeth may *understand,* all that is required of him to make him holy, and to make him happy. Yet, I know not how it happens, whether from carelessness or perverseness, or both; the plainest and most interesting truths are sometimes overlooked and disregarded, and at other times mistaken, or perverted. Even the doctrine in the text, though so often held forth, and so earnestly inculcated, in the New Testament, has been strangely passed over by some pretended preachers of the gospel; and a shorter way to heaven has been pointed out by false guides, quite different from that shown us by Christ and his apostles. But, my "little children" (I speak to you in the words of scripture) " let no man deceive you: he that *doeth* righteousness, *is* righteous." And " without holiness," or righteousness, "no man shall see the Lord." " If thou wilt enter into life," says our Saviour, " KEEP THE COMMANDMENTS." And again : "Blessed are they that hear the word of God : and KEEP it." In like manner, says St. Paul : "God will render to every man ACCORDING TO HIS DEEDS: glory, honour, and peace" (that is, *eternal* glory and happiness) " to every man that WORKETH GOOD." And in

another

another epiftle, "WORK OUT your own falvation." So alfo St. James: "Be ye DOERS of the
word, and not hearers only," for "faith without
works is dead." And St. John, in the Revela-
tion: "Bleffed are they that DO HIS COMMAND-
MENTS, that they may have right to the Tree
of Life."—Thefe texts (to which many more
might be added) are fo exceedingly plain and
clear, that you cannot fail, I think, to underftand them. And the matter of them is fo important, that they deferve your utmoft attention
and conftant remembrance. Confider, I befeech
you, the end and defign of Chrift's coming into
the world. It was, "that he might redeem us
from all iniquity, and purify unto himfelf a peculiar," or holy, "people, zealous of good
works;" that, being fully inftructed by him in
the will of God, we "might ferve him, in holinefs and righteoufnefs all the days of our life."
"This is a faithful faying," fays St. Paul,
"that Chrift Jefus came into the world to
fave finners." Very true. But *how* did he fave
them? Not only by offering himfelf a facrifice
for fins paft, but alfo by reforming, and leading
them to obedience for the future; "teaching
them, that denying ungodlinefs and worldly
lufts, they fhould live foberly, righteoufly, and
godly, in this prefent world." "*This*," therefore
(as the fame apoftle declares) is *likewife* "a
faithful faying, that they which have *believed*
in God might be careful to MAINTAIN GOOD
WORKS; that is, to live fuitably to their belief
and profeffion. Religion is an *active* fervice.
It is not enough, that it be rooted in the heart,
                                              and

and shew itself in outward professions of faith
and godliness: it must also bring forth the *fruit*
of good works. These are the only sure evi-
dences of it; and to these only are its rewards
and promises annexed. To call Christ our Lord
and Master, and not obey his commands, is no
better than a mockery of him; an affront and
insult to him. *Practical* infidels (such, I mean,
as acknowledge Christ with their *mouths*, but in
their *works* deny him) are the worst of all infidels. We cannot plead ignorance of our duty;
for he has fully and clearly revealed it to us.
We cannot plead inability to perform it; for he
has graciously promised the assistance of his
Holy Spirit to all that ask for it. Tho' weak
of ourselves, we can " do all things," necessary
to our salvation, " thro' Christ that strengthen-
eth us." If therefore we fail in our duty, we
are wholly without excuse. In vain shall we
cry, Lord, Lord, either here or hereafter, if we
do not approve ourselves his faithful and obedient servants. In vain shall we sue for mercy,
when he comes to judgment: when his answer
will be, " I never knew you: depart from me,
ye that work iniquity."

By what has been said of the necessity of doing the will of God, in order to obtain the rewards of heaven, you are not to suppose that
our good actions have any *merit* in them, or that
we properly *deserve* those rewards.—No.—
" Eternal life is the *gift*," the free undeserved
gift " of God, through Jesus Christ our Lord."
It is his merits, and all-perfect obedience, that
must recommend our imperfect services to God.
There

There is therefore no room "for boasting" on *our* part.—Far otherwise.—But if with faith and humility, we do the best we can to serve and please God, we may be sure that our services, however imperfect, will be accepted; and that, however undeserving, we shall not "lose our reward."

ADMONITION XII.

GALATIANS vi. 7—former part.

Be not deceived; God is not mocked.

ALAS! how liable are we to be deceived by others; and, what is still worse, how apt are we to deceive ourselves! This perhaps may seem strange; but it is too true, and too easily accounted for. Besides deceivers and enemies *without*; evil men and evil spirits, that are ever watching to seduce us; we have an enemy no less dangerous lurking *within*, that is continually ready to betray us. For " THE HEART," says the prophet, " IS DECEITFUL ABOVE ALL THINGS, and desperately wicked: who can know it?" Who can find out its dark windings and turnings; its secret arts and impositions; its deceitful workings; whereby we are continually in danger of being misled from our duty, and drawn into sin? Against every kind of deceit, whereby our salvation is endangered, we have frequent cautions and admonitions in the holy scriptures, and particularly in the epistles of St. Paul. In one place we read: " Let no man deceive you with vain words."

In

In another; " Let no man deceive *himself.*"
In the text; " Be not deceived"—which may
be underſtood as a warning againſt both kinds
of deceit; from others as well as from ourſelves.
The very ſame words are uſed by St. James,
tho' differently tranſlated; where he ſays; " Do
not *err,* my beloved brethren." For error will
be the conſequence of deceit in either caſe;
whether it proceed from within or without.
After this general admonition, " Be not deceived;" it follows: " God is not mocked."
As if the Apoſtle had ſaid; " Beware of being
deceived, or of deceiving yourſelves. For tho'
you may impoſe upon yourſelves, or upon one
another, you cannot deceive or impoſe upon
God." The very notion, the expreſſion, of
mocking God, carries with it ſomething ſhock-
ing and profane. And yet every wilful ſin is, in
ſome ſort, an attempt to mock God; and every
wilful ſinner is, in ſome ſenſe, guilty of this
horrid blaſphemy. The language of his heart
(if not of his mouth) is thus deſcribed by the
Pſalmiſt; " How doth God know? is there
knowledge in the Moſt High?" And again;
" God hath forgotten: he hideth his face, he will
never ſee it." Such is the folly and deceitful-
neſs, of ſin; blinding the underſtanding, at the
ſame time that it corrupts the heart. To ſuch
falſe reaſonings, ſuch abſurd ſuppoſitions, is the
ſinner driven. Various are the arts and delu-
ſions, by which men impoſe upon themſelves,
and upon one another. But the moſt general
and common way is, by an imagination, that
they may be ſaved, or go to heaven, without

leading

leading a good and holy life—than which nothing can be more directly contrary to the plain
and conftant doctrine of fcripture, and particularly of the New Teftament. Our Saviour fays
exprefsly; that " he only who doeth the will of
God, fhall enter into his heavenly kingdom"—
that, if we will enter into life, we *muft* " keep
the commandments." The fame important
truth is continually held forth to us by his
Apoftles. " Whatfoever a man foweth," fays
St. Paul, " that fhall he alfo reap"—" Without holinefs no man fhall fee the Lord."—It is
as impoffible to get to heaven without a life of
good works, as it is to have a good crop of corn
without fowing good feed; or to "gather grapes
of thorns, or figs of thiftles."—Let no one therefore deceive you with vain pretences, and falfe
hopes of falvation, contrary to the exprefs word
of God.—Read your Bible; believe it; act according to it; and you cannot think or act amifs.
Does a Gofpel-preacher (as he falfely calls himfelf) tell you that faith alone will fave you? that
if you truft to the merits of Chrift, that will be
fufficient?—anfwer him, in the words of Scripture, that " faith without works is dead;"
and that " by works a man is juftified, and not
by faith only."—Tell him, that you believe,
and truft, in the merits of your Saviour as firmly
and fincerely as he can do; but that, without an
holy and good life on *your* part, thofe merits will
be of no avail to you: for that Chrift "gave
himfelf for us, that he might redeem us from all
iniquity, and purify unto himfelf a peculiar" (or
holy) " people, zealous of good works."

Again:

Again: Take great care that you be not deceived by idle and worthless companions, who
will use all their arts and frauds to corrupt both
your principles and manners.—Do not converse
with such—turn away from them;—fly from
them as you would from a plague, or other con-
tagious distemper.— They are "fools," in Solomon's judgment, that " make a mock at sin:"
and they are *worse* than fools, that would argue,
or laugh, you out of your religion and virtue.

Lastly: Beware of your own hearts;—never
flatter yourselves that you are in the way of salvation, while you are in the way of sin or wickedness, and let me advise you often and fer-
vently to pray in the words of David; " Search
me, O God, and know my heart; try me, and
know my thoughts—and see if there be any wicked way in me; and lead me in the way everlasting."

ADMONITION XIII.

PHILIPPIANS i. 27.

*Let your conversation be as it becometh the gospel of
Christ.*

THE word " conversation," here, as well
as in other parts of the Bible, does not
signify our talk or discourse; but takes in the
whole of our conduct and behaviour in life: so
that we are to understand the precept in the text
as a general injunction to live as becomes Christians; to conform ourselves in all things to the
excellent rules and directions laid down in the
gospel of Christ; to be "holy, (as St. Peter
expresses it) " in all manner of conversation."
The

The neceffity of this, in order to our falvation, is fo very plain and evident, both from reafon and fcripture, and has been fo fully fhewn to you in a former difcourfe, that I fhall not repeat what I faid upon that fubject: but fhall rather point out to you fome particulars, in which we fhould be more that ordinarily careful to follow the direction in the text; and fo approve our-felves *real* Chriftians, and fincere difciples of him whofe name we bear, and by whom we hope to be faved.

Now "the wifdom that is from above," or the religion which Chrift came down from heaven to teach us, "is firft pure:" that is, it requires great purity of heart as well as of man-ners—what the Pfalmift calls "a clean heart," and "clean hands"—ftrict chaftity in all our thoughts, words, and actions. "For this ye know," fays the apoftle (and I earneftly befeech you always to bear it in remembrance), "that no unclean perfon hath any inheritance in the kingdom of Chrift and of God."

Again: it is "peaceable, gentle, and eafy to be intreated." The gofpel, like its divine au-thor, breathes the fpirit of love, peace, and be-nevolence, in every part of it. "By this," fays our Saviour, "fhall all men know that ye are my difciples, if ye have love one to another." You fee, he makes it the diftinguifhing mark, or badge, of our profeffion. And, as a peace-able difpofition and behaviour is the natural fruit of love, fo we are commanded to "have peace one with another;—to "live in peace," or "peaceably with all men;"—to "feek peace,

3   and

and enfue it;"—with many more exhortations
to the fame purpofe.——Gentlenefs is another
Chriftian grace, or virtue, fpringing from love.
It fignifies a meek and quiet fpirit, a mild temper of mind, that fhews itfelf in a fuitable behaviour; kind, affable, and courteous. "I befeech you," fays St. Paul, "by the meeknefs
and gentlenefs of Chrift :" which qualities he
particularly recommends, in another place, to
the imitation of his difciples; where he fays,
"Put them in mind to be gentle, fhewing all
meeknefs unto all men."—Another mark of a
true Chriftian temper is, that it is "eafy to be
intreated;"—obliging, complying, and ready to
forgive injuries and offences. The great duty
of forgivenefs our Lord lays a very particular
ftrefs upon, as abfolutely and indifpenfably neceffary to our being forgiven by God. What
words can be plainer, or ftronger, to this effect,
than what he ufes immediately after the prayer
he teaches his difciples ; "If ye forgive men
their trefpaffes, your heavenly Father will alfo
forgive *you.* But if ye forgive not men *their*
trefpaffes, neither will your father forgive *your*
trefpaffes." And in his parable of the merci-
lefs fervant (Matt. xviii.) he enforces the fame
doctrine in terms no lefs clear and powerful.
The gofpel wifdom of the Chriftian fpirit is
alfo "full of mercy and good fruits;" prompt-
ing us to every act of humanity and compaf-
fion, to fhew our love in actual fervices to all
within our reach ; following the example of our
bleffed Mafter, who "went about doing good."
—Laftly; it is "without partiality, and without
hypocrify."

C

hypocrisy." The true Christian is open, sincere, honest; free from every narrow selfish view, from all undue prejudice and partiality. His love is " without dissimulation." His words flow from his heart; and his actions correspond with his words.

I have here given you a short sketch of Christian virtue, or of such a conversation as " becomes the gospel of Christ." A more particular account of its relative, or social, duties, you will find admirably drawn up in your Catechism, in that article which describes your duty towards your neighbour. Let me beg of you often to look at it, and to consider it with attention: a better lesson you cannot have, nor can you follow a better guide. Think of it every day of your lives; and practise it conscientiously. Indeed the *whole* Catechism is so excellent, that I would wish you to make it your constant companion through life. Do not forget or despise it, as if it were fit only for the use of *children:* it is fit for *every* age; as it contains the sum and substance of the Christian religion.

There is one quality, or disposition, which both our Saviour and his apostles, in a very particular manner, recommend, and require as absolutely necessary to a disciple of Christ; which is, heavenly-mindedness:— to " set our affections on things above;" to make heaven the principal end of our thoughts and pursuits. For, as St. Paul expresses it, " our conversation is in heaven"—*there* lies our true interest—*that* is the country to which we belong—*there* is our treasure—

5

treasure—*there*, then, should our " hearts be
also." If they are so, if we are sincere and in-
earnest in our religion, we shall not fail to fulfil
the precept in the text; we shall consider ourselves as strangers, or travellers, upon earth; and
our " conversation" *here* will be " such as becometh the gospel of Christ."

ADMONITION XIV.

ROMANS xii. 11—former part.

Not slothful in Business.

NEVER BE IDLE—sloth, or idleness, is the
ruin and destruction both of body and
soul. It is not only a great evil in itself, but it
is productive also of many other evils. It leads
to sickness, poverty, sensuality, dishonesty, and
loss of character. It is unnatural: for we are
by nature formed for action, and fond of it. It
is contrary to our duty and obligation as men,
or social creatures; who were made to help, and
do good to, one another. It is contrary to the
express will and command of God; who has
taught and directed us, in his holy word, to be
diligent and industrious, active and laborious,
in our several callings; and to be continually
employed in serving and assisting our brethren.
The misery and sinfulness of a slothful and idle
life, and the blessings of an industrious one, are
set before us in very strong terms, in many pas-
sages of holy scripture. " Slothfulness," says
the wise man, " casteth into a deep sleep, and
an idle soul shall suffer hunger." " The soul

C 2   of

of the fluggard defireth, and hath nothing: but
the foul of the diligent fhall be made fat." "The
hand of the diligent maketh rich," but " the
defire of the flothful killeth him." " In all
labour there is profit," not only in this life, but
our "works," we are affured, will " follow" us
into that which is to come; there to meet with
their full reward: where, on the other hand,
" the unprofitable fervant;" he who has wafted
his time here in idlenefs, and made no ufe or
improvement of the talents committed to his
truft; fhall be " caft into outer darknefs," and
punifhed with eternal mifery.—In the text, as
well as in many other parts of his Epiftles, St.
Paul warns us againft the fin of idlenefs, and exhorts us to the oppofite virtue of induftry. For
when he forbids us to be flothful, he plainly bids
us be diligent; as he commands his difciples, in
another place, to " work with their own hands,"
and to " labour, working the thing which is
good :" and again, " if any will not work,"
fays he, " neither fhould he eat." The words,
" Not flothful in bufinefs," imply thefe two
things: firft, that we have all fome bufinefs to
do; fome work, fome calling, that we ought to
be employed in; and, fecondly, that we fhould
be active and induftrious in following it.—Our
all wife and good Creator has defigned and
fitted us for action and labour, both of body and
mind. He has made it neceffary to our own
well being, as individuals; and likewife to the
good of fociety, as we are focial creatures, or
" members one of another." Various and different are the tafks allotted us; as are the abi-
lities

ſities and opportunſties we are furniſhed with of
performing them. High and low, rich and
poor, old and young, learned and unlearned, we
have all ſome work aſſigned us, which it is our
duty to do, both for ourſelves, and for one another. Some are to work with their hands, ſome
with their head, and ſome with both. Our ſeveral ſituations in life plainly point out to us,
what it is our duty to be employed in. Our
principal concern is, to be diligent in that employment. " Whatſoever thy hand," or thy
head, " findeth to do, do it with thy might."
Exert all your ſtrength, uſe all your diligence,
in the execution of it. Loſe no time, ſpare no
pains, in learning, and in doing, your duty.——
You, my good children, are more particularly
obliged to be induſtrious in your ſeveral occu-
pations—you have had great advantages in being taught your duty; you are therefore doubly
bound to practiſe it. While *we* are working
with our *heads* for *your* good, *you* are without
excuſe if you do not work diligently with your
hands for *your own*—while *our* time is employed
in inſtructing you, it is *your* buſineſs and duty to
profit by our inſtructions. You are young, and
healthy, and able to work: and your ſtation in
life is ſuch as requires you ſo to do for your bread
and ſupport. It is your duty alſo to work for your
parents, and occaſionally for your other friends
and benefactors. And believe me, it is as much
your intereſt and your happineſs, as it is your
duty, to be always well employed. It will give
you health of body, and peace of mind. It will
make your days cheerful and comfortable, and

your

your sleep of nights sweet and refreshing. It will make you beloved and esteemed by all that know you. It will enable you to provide, not only for yourselves, but for your families likewise, when you have any. It will make you useful members of society; good neighbours, and valuable friends.—By your *example*, at least, you may all do good; and in some sort fulfil the precept of our blessed Saviour, to " let your light so shine before men, that they may see your good works, and glorify your Father which is in heaven."

And here let me give you one caution: that while you are discharging your duty towards *men*, you do not forget your duty towards God. Indeed by doing the one, you are in a great measure discharging the other. But what I mean is, that you never let the duties of your several stations or employments in life, so far take up your time and thoughts, as to hinder you from praying to God, and paying him the worship that is due to him, both in private and public. For remember, that no labour or business can prosper without *his* blessing attending it; and that the same commandment which permits, and enjoins, our working for *six* days, requires us to " keep holy" the seventh; that, as we should be employed chiefly on the other days in providing for our *bodily* and *temporal* wants, so on the sabbath, or Lord's day, we should labour for our *spiritual* sustenance; for that " meat which endureth unto everlasting life."

ADMONI-

ADMONITION XV.

EPHESIANS vi. 7 and 8.

With good will doing service, as to the Lord, and not to men: knowing that whatsoever good thing any man doeth, the same shall he receive of the Lord, whether he be bond or free.

WE are here, as well as in other parts of the epistles, instructed in the duty of servants to their masters and mistresses. For the scripture, being a rule of life and manners, as well as of faith, gives us directions, not only for our duty in general, but also for the discharge of every branch of it in particular; according to our different callings and situations. Now, as many of you may probably go to service in some part of your life, some rules for your good behaviour therein may be of use and benefit to you; and such I mean at present to lay before you.

In the text you may observe, first, a general direction given you, *how* to do your duty as servants properly and conscientiously: and secondly, a *reward* held forth to you as an encouragement for so doing—Let us consider each distinctly—The rule is this—"With good-will doing service, as to the Lord, and not to men." "With good-will," signifies, with a willing and ready mind; with an affectionate and obliging disposition; with a desire to please "not by constraint, but willingly," and cheerfully.—And it is to be done, " as to the Lord, and not to men,"—that is, from a *religious* prin-

ciple,

ciple, or a fenfe of duty towards God. As the apoftle elfewhere expreffes it; "not with eye-fer-vice, as men-pleafers, but in finglenefs of heart, fearing God"—" and whatfoever ye do, do it heartily, as to the Lord, and not unto men."—The meaning is, not that we are to *overlook* our duty and obligations to men; but that we are to *look farther*, to the fountain and origin of all duty, which is the will and command of God: and that, while we ferve our mafters *on earth*, we fhould confider ourfelves as doing fervice to CHRIST, who is our mafter *in heaven*.—" Not with eye-fervice, as men-pleafers,"—that is, not barely endeavouring to pleafe, and gain the good-will of, our mafters, by doing what we think they will like, when their eyes are *upon* us: but ferving them truly and faithfully at *all* times, when they are *abfent*, as well as *pre-fent*—" as the fervants of Chrift," who always fees what we are doing—" in finglenefs of heart"—that is fincerely and confcientioufly—"fearing God," and " doing his will from the heart;"—always remembering, that he fearcheth our hearts, and knoweth our inward thoughts, and moft fecret defigns, as well as our outward ac-tions; and that he will reward, or punifh, us, according as they are good, or bad, in his fight. Whatfoever therefore we do, in the fervice of our mafters and miftreffes, we are to do it " heartily," and " with a good-will," as unto God, and unto Chrift—to whom we are ac-countable for our behaviour, in this, as well as in every other part of our duty towards man. The fame direction that David gave his fon Solomon

lomon for the service of God, will hold good for
the service of our earthly masters—" Serve
him," says he, " with a perfect heart, and with
a willing mind."—The truth is, that without a
willing disposition, and a sincere desire of doing
our duty, nothing can be done as it ought. A
good-will is the great spring of action. A ready
and cheerful mind is the great support of it. It
gives vigour to our faculties, quickens our diligence, and enables us to overcome many diffi-
culties. It makes the discharge of our duty both
easy and pleasant to us. In service, as well as
in every other situation of life, the best rule we
can go by is what St. Paul lays down for the
giving of alms; to act " not grudgingly, or of
necessity"—and for the same reason he men-
tions— " for God," says he, " loveth a cheerful
giver."—So we may say no less truly; God
loveth a servant, who does his duty cheerfully,
and willingly.— And we may add, he will reward
him accordingly. For so the apostle goes on
in the text; " knowing," says he, " that whatsoever good thing any man doth, the same shall
he receive of the Lord, whether he be bond or
free." God, who is " no respecter of persons,"
will most assuredly reward every man, without
distinction, according to his deeds.—Our stations and allotments in *this* life are indeed very
different, and the good things of it (as they are
called) are unequally distributed. But the trea-
sures of the *next*, the riches and blessings of
heaven, are open to all alike :—with regard to
them, it matters not what our condition is here
in this world ;—if we do but our duty in that

state

state of life to which God has called us, we are sure of being happy hereafter, beyond all we can hope or conceive, to all eternity. Whether high or low, rich or poor, " bond or free," it makes no difference. We are all alike under God's notice; all equally accountable to him for our actions and behaviour; and all equally sure of being rewarded by him for our good conduct, or punished for our bad. The good and faithful servant, who acts from a religious principle, and with a willing mind; who serves his master honestly, and diligently; doing his duty to the best of his knowledge and ability; will generally find his account, and be rewarded, *in this world*. But be that as it may, he is certain that his services will not be forgotten or unrewarded in the *next*: where he will " enter into the joy of his Lord," and partake of it for ever and ever.

ADMONITION XVI.

TITUS ii. 9 and 10.

'Exhort servants to be obedient unto their own masters, and to please them well in all things : not answering again; not purloining; but shewing all good fidelity : that they may adorn the doctrine of God our Saviour in all things.

HAVING considered the duty of servants in general, we will now take a view of the several branches of it in particular. And for this purpose we cannot have a better guide than the exhortation of the Apostle in the text; which

which shews us both what is to be done, and
what is to be avoided. In the first place, servants are " to be obedient unto their own mafters,"—and of courfe to their miftreffes; the
fame obligation binding them to one, as to the
other: fo that when one only is named, we are
to underftand, and apply the direction to, both.
Now the very notion of fervitude implies obedience. It is the mafter's part, to command;
the fervant's, to obey. You muft always do
what your mafter or miftrefs bids you. You
muft not difpute their orders, becaufe you fancy
them unreafonable, or hard to comply with; but
you muft endeavour to execute them in the beft
manner you can. When they tell you to do a
thing *one* way, you muft not attempt to do it
another; becaufe perhaps you think it eafier or
quicker.—No, they are much better judges than
you, and they are the only proper judges how
to have their own bufinefs done. It is your
duty to do it as they direct; without murmuring, or difputing. You fhould obey them willingly, readily, and cheerfully; ufing your beft
endeavours (as the text directs) " to pleafe them
well in all things." You fhould not be content
with barely following orders; with doing juft
what is required of you, and no more. You
fhould be careful to do every thing in the beft
manner, and with the greateft difpatch, in your
power; to fhew that you take a pleafure in
obliging thofe, whom you are bound to ferve.
For this end you fhould not always wait for *re-
ceiving* their orders; but endeavour to be *before-
hand* with them, in doing what you think will

pleafe

pleafe them. A free and voluntary fervice is doubly pleafing and acceptable. To do what we are commanded, is an act of ftrict duty, as paying a debt is of ftrict juftice. But to do a piece of fervice of our own accord, without being bid, is like a free gift, and will be valued accordin_y. But don't miftake me. Though I compare it to a free gift, it is ftill our duty to *pleafe*, as well as to *obey*: as it is, in like manner, our duty to be *generous*, as well as *juft*. And if you have but a defire and inclination, you will never want opportunities of pleafing thofe you ferve. Let it be your conftant ftudy and delight fo to do.———The text now informs us, what we are *not* to do—" not anfwering again—not purloining." To anfwer again, fignifies, to contradict, to argue, or difpute, a point with a mafter or miftrefs—or to give them pert and faucy anfwers. Thefe are great faults, contrary to all the rules of good manners, contrary to the duty of fervants; which I charge you to avoid. When you are fpoken to, the lefs you fay, the better. Receive your orders filently and fubmiffively. When you are told of your faults, make no reply, except to fay, you are forry for having offended, and that you will do fo no more.—And be fure to *do* as you *promife*. It is by actions, not by words, that you muft fhew your forrow, and your amendment. After, " not anfwering again," follows, " not purloining." By " purloining," is meant every fort of theft, or difhonefty; which is not only a breach of duty, but a moft abominable fin; every kind and degree of which you muft keep

clear

clear of, as you value your character, your life, or your salvation. In this, as in other sins, *little* offences lead to *great* ones; and he that begins with cheating and pilfering, will in time proceed to the higher crimes of theft and robbery, and most likely end his life at the gallows. Beware, therefore, I intreat you, of the first beginnings of this sin. Never take what belongs to another, be the thing ever so small or trifling. And particularly, never meddle with what belongs to your master or mistress; for this is a double crime; a breach of trust, as well as dishonesty. For you are required not only to serve and obey them, but (as the text goes on to instruct us) to shew them " all good fidelity"—that is, to be strictly faithful to them in the management of all their concerns—to make *their* interest your *own*—in short, to do by *them*, as you would they should do unto *you*, were you in their place, and they in your's.—This takes in a large compass of duty, and compleats the character of a good servant. Be faithful to them, therefore, in *every* thing—to their property, by making no waste, and improving every thing to the utmost of your power—and to their good name and reputation, by always speaking handsomely of them, and taking their part, if at any time you hear them slandered or abused. And as you are to serve them faithfully and obediently yourselves, so you are to use your best persuasions, and endeavours, to make your fellow-servants do the same.

The text concludes with a motive, or encouragement, to servants, for their general good behaviour:

behaviour: " that they may adorn the doctrine
of God our Saviour in all things"—that is, that
by doing their duty in that state of life to which
they are called, they may be an ornament to
their profession, and do credit to the religion
which teaches it.—But of this more in my next.

ADMONITION XVII.

TITUS ii. 10.—latter part.

———*That they may adorn the doctrine of God
our Saviour in all things.*

THE Apostle having laid down several excellent rules and directions to servants for
the due discharge of their duty, enforces the ob-
servance of them from this powerful considera-
tion; "that they may adorn the doctrine of God
our Saviour in all things." By " the doctrine
of God our Saviour," we are to understand the
religion of Christ: and whoever lives suitably
to that religion, and regulates his life and behaviour by its holy laws and precepts, is said to
" adorn" it; that is, to bring credit to it, or to
be an ornament to his profession—a shining
light, whereby others may be directed and led
to follow his good example. And this is in the
power of every Christian, without exception.
Let his station in life be what it will, if he lives
agreeably to it, and conscientiously performs the
duties it requires, he may be said to *adorn* the
doctrine or religion he professes: as, on the
other hand, whoever lives unsuitably to his profession, whatever outward ornaments he may be
distinguished

distinguished by, is a shame and disgrace to it; bringing a reproach, and scandal, on that holy name by which he is called. By " breaking the law," he is said to " dishonour God." So that it is not our rank or situation in life, but our good or bad behaviour in that situation, which is properly an ornament or disgrace to us. By doing our duty, we may adorn the *lowest*; by transgressing it, we may disgrace the *highest*. And this surely should be a great encouragement to servants to be active, and diligent, and faithful, in the discharge of their duty; as well as a great comfort to them, when they consider that they are thereby adorning the religion in which that duty is taught; that they bring credit, not to themselves only, but to their holy profession likewise; that by serving their earthly masters faithfully, they are doing an acceptable service to their master in heaven: that by promoting the interest of one, they are serving the cause of the other. Think, therefore, my good children, how much depends on your behaviour, and what you have to answer for, when you go into service: not only your own credit and reputation, but also that of the religion you have been brought up, and so carefully instructed, in, —which you will either recommend and promote by your good example, or disgrace and disparage by your bad one. And be not ashamed of your condition, as if it were mean and disgraceful. There is nothing mean but vice and sin; nothing shameful but wickedness and disobedience. A bad servant is indeed a scandal to his profession, and a pest of society: a good
one

one is an ornament of the one, and a valuable member of the other. Look into your bible, and there you will fee what is the true ornament of a Chriftian:—not *outward* fhow and finery, but that of " a meek and quiet fpirit;" which, we are told, " is in the fight of God of great price;" and which is, in a peculiar manner, the diftinguifhing mark and character of a good fer- vant. Our bleffed Mafter, who, though he was Lord of all, " took upon him the form of a fer- vant," that we might follow the example of his great humility, left this admirable leffon to all his difciples: " Learn of me," faye he; " for I am meek and lowly in heart." And if he, though he was the Son of God " learned," and practif d, " obedience" to man; furely *we* are doubly bound to obey thofe who are fet over us, and to ferve them truly and faithfully, as we are the fervants of Chrift.

Before I have done, I muft defire your parti- cular attention to the laft words of the text— " *in all things* ;" which imply, that our obedience to the commands of God, in whatever ftation we a?e, muft be *general*, and *univerfal*. If we would adorn our profeffion, we muft conform ourfelves to it *in all things:* our *whole* life and converfa- tion muft be " fuch as becometh the gofpel of Chrift." We muft ufe our beft endeavours to improve, and excel, in *every* part of our duty; that, as St. James expreffes it, we " may be per- fect and intire, wanting nothing." For if we neglect any duty, or indulge ourfelves in the practice of any vice or fin, we are a difgrace to our holy religion, and deferve not the name of Chriftians.

Chriftians. God, of his infinite mercy and goodnefs, has indeed offered " falvation unto all men"
through Chrift Jefus; but it is upon this exprefs
condition, that " denying," or renouncing, all
" ungodlinefs and wordly lufts, we fhould live
foberly, righteoufly, and godly, in this prefent
world;" or, in the words of the text, that we
fhould "adorn the doctrine of God our Saviour
in all things;"—always remembering, that the
fame divine Perfon who once came from heaven
to *fave* the world, will hereafter come to *judge*
it; to call every one of us to account for our
behaviour, and to reward or punifh us according
to our deeds. And God grant that this confideration may have its due weight and influence
on us all! that in whatever ftation of life his
providence fhall place us, we may do the duties
of that ftation faithfully and confcientioufly;—
not murmuring or repining, but content and
thankful to the Giver of all goodnefs;—keeping conftantly in view " the end of our faith,"
and obedience; " even the SALVATION OF OUR
SOULS."

ADMONITION XVIII.

1 TIMOTHY vi. 6.

Godlinefs with contentment is great gain.

THE defire of gain is common to moft
people; and if properly directed, and
kept within due bounds, it ferves as a fpur to
induftry, and ought not to be difcouraged. But
let me afk, *What is gain?* and how is it to be
acquired?

acquired? Does it confist merely in wealth, and what are called the good things of *this* life? No; thefe are but a fmall portion of it; of inferior value, and of very uncertain tenure; and fhould therefore be but the *fecondary* objects of our purfuit. In order to judge rightly, and act properly, in this bufinefs, let us confult the word of God. " WISDOM," fays Solomon (by which he always means religion, or godlinefs) " is the principal thing, therefore GET WISDOM; and with all thy getting GET UNDERSTANDING." And the apoftle, in the text, tells us, that " godlinefs with contentment is great gain." *Without* it, all the riches in the world could give us no real comfort or happinefs; and *with* it, we cannot fail to be happy even in the loweft and pooreft condition. " The merchandife of it is better than the merchandife of filver, and the gain thereof than fine gold." It is a "pearl of great price;" a treafure of ineftimable value; which we may all obtain if we pleafe. We cannot all be rich, or great: but we may all be godly: we may all be contented.———Let us confider the text a little more particularly: it will afford us much matter of ufeful inftruction.

The word " godlinefs," fignifies properly the fame as piety, or a right difpofition of the heart towards God. But we may look upon it here as including the *whole* of our duty, which indeed naturally flows from a truly pious heart. For whoever fincerely loves God, will love his brother alfo; and will endeavour to ferve and pleafe God by a general obedience to all his commandments.

commandments. Now one great part of our duty, is contentment; fo that there can be no true godlinefs without it. The apoftle therefore joins them together, and recommends them under the notion of "great gain" or profit: as he fays in another part of the fame epiftle, that " godlinefs is *profitable* unto *all* things"—it is the greateft gain we can be poffeffed of—" having" (as he goes on to inform us) " promife of the life that now is, and of that which is to come." The advantages attending it in this life are many and great. Generally, health of body; and always, peace of mind. A good name, which, Solomon fays, " is rather to be chofen than great riches;" and oftentimes a good fhare of wealth befides. And in the next life the gain is certain, and unfpeakably great. " To him that foweth righteoufnefs fhall be a SURE REWARD."

Again: as godlinefs, in general, is reprefented by the apoftle as fo gainful and beneficial to us; fo that particular part of it, " contentment," as he plainly intimates, contributes not a little to the profits attending it. " A good man" (who muft be a contented man) " is fatisfied from himfelf." He has a fource of comfort within him, independent of fortune, and of all outward accidents or circumftances, that never fails him. His wants are few, and they are eafily fupplied. His defires are moderate, and they are foon fatisfied. He wifely confiders that as he " brought nothing into this world, it is certain he can carry nothing out." " Having food and raiment, he is therewith content;"

thankful,

thankful, and happy. A ftranger to the cares
of covetoufnefs, the pangs of ambition, and the
tortures of envy; he enjoys what he has, nor is
eagerly folicitous for more. Ever trufting in
the gracious providence and love of Him, who
has promifed that he will never leave, or forfake,
his faithful fervants.

You fee, then, what is the *true* intereft of man;
the " GREAT GAIN," which he ought always to
have in view, and to purfue with his utmoft care
and diligence. You may obferve, too, how St.
Paul, in imitation of his bleffed Mafter, takes
every opportunity of pointing it out to us, and
of exhorting us to "follow after godlinefs;" and,
after his own example, " in whatfoever ftate we
are, therewith to be content." But you are
not to fuppofe that either our Saviour, or his
apoftle, forbids a *moderate* attention to what we
call our *worldly* intereft, or a well-regulated purfuit of *worldly gain.* " Seek ye *firft* the kingdom
of God and his righteoufnefs," plainly directs
us to make religion, and the bleffings of heaven,
our *principal* care and concern; but as plainly
allows us, in a fecond and fubordinate view, to
attend to the good things of *this* life. Labour
and induftry in our worldly callings are not only
permitted, but enjoined, us. He that neglects
to " provide for his own houfhold," or family,
is, in St. Paul's judgment, " worfe than an in-
fidel." We are directed to be " *content* with
food and raiment;" that is, with the bare ne-
ceffaries of life; but we are not forbid to ufe
our honeft endeavours to obtain the comforts
and conveniences of it. In a word, we are allowed

lowed to *use* this world, and the good things of it, so as we do not *abuse* them: remembering always, that our true and lasting treasure is in heaven. And where our treasure is, there may our hearts be also.

ADMONITION XIX.
REVELATION xxi. 8—latter part.

ALL LIARS *shall have their part in the lake which burneth with fire and brimstone: which is the second death.*

EVERY sin is an offence against God, and exposes the sinner to his anger and punishment. But there are some sins particularly hateful to him, and which will be punished by him with more than ordinary severity. Of this sort is lying. It is a sin above all others vile and abominable, as it proceeds from a most wicked and corrupt heart, and is in a particular manner the work of the Devil, who is called " a liar, and the father of lies." And accordingly we find it in scripture spoken of in the strongest terms of detestation; and all liars ranked with the very worst sort of sinners, and subjected to the severest wrath and vengeance of God.—" Lying lips," says Solomon, " are abomination to the Lord." And in the text you may observe, liars are joined with " murderers, and whoremongers, and forcerers, and idolaters;" and are doomed to partake of their punishment in the world to come. And again, in the same chapter ver. 27, it is written; " There shall
in

in no wife enter into it" (that is, into heaven) " any thing that defileth, neither whatfoever worketh abomination, or MAKETH A LIE." And again, Ch. xxii. 15, " Without," (that is, in hell) " are dogs, and forcerers, and whore-mongers, and murderers, and idolaters, and *whofoever loveth and maketh a lie.*" It is ob-fervable that liars and murderers are here put together, forafmuch as lying and murder are two of the moft heinous fins, and as they both proceed from the devil, and make men refemble him, more perhaps than any other fins whatever. For the devil (as our Saviour tells us) " was a murderer from the beginning," as well as " a liar;" as he by his lies caufed our firft pa-rents to commit that fin, which brought death upon them and their pofterity. So that as he was the father of lies, he was, properly fpeak-ing, the author of death, or the murderer of mankind. And whoever follows him in his wicked practices, and particularly in this worft of wickednefs, lying; will moft affuredly fhare with him in his punifhment, and will have that dreadful fentence pronounced on him at the day of judgment; " Depart from me, ye curfed, into everlafting fire, prepared for the devil and his angels"—which is what is called in the text " the *fecond death*"—and is always fpoken of in fcripture as a ftate of continual torment, and of extreme and endlefs mifery. But it is not in the *next* world only that liars are punifhed. They commonly, if not always, fuffer feverely in *this*. Lying is above all other fins hateful to man, as well as to God. Other offenders often meet with pity,
and

and sometimes with favour more than they deserve; but liars are hated by every body without distinction, and shunned as the vilest of
wretches, and the pests of society. Hear what
the Psalmist says of them. " I hate and abhor
lying. He that worketh deceit, shall not dwell
within my house: he that telleth lies, shall not
tarry in my sight." And the reason of it is
plain. For lying shews a most wicked and depraved heart, a mean and base spirit, a disposition to all manner of fraud and iniquity.—Other
sinners may have some good qualities to recommend them: a liar has none. Against other
bad persons we may be upon our guard: but
one is never safe with a liar, His " throat is an
open sepulchre: the poison of asps is under his
lips." And he spreads his poison far and wide,
wherever he goes. His delight is to do mischief,
to destroy characters, and to breed quarrels and
dissensions. No wonder then that so base and
wicked a creature should be despised and ab-
horred by every body; and that the name of
liar should be reckoned the greatest mark of in-
famy and reproach that any person can bear.

And now, my good children, *think* only (God
forbid you should ever *know*) what a life a liar
must lead, and what he must feel—mistrusted;
never believed, not even if he speaks truth;
despised, scorned, hated, by all mankind. Always in danger, always in fear, of being found
out, and meeting with the due reward of his
wickedness. No friend to help or comfort him
in his distress; and the pangs of a guilty conscience continually tormenting him—till at last
death

death delivers him over to the heaviest and severest punishments of the world to come.

"Wherefore," to use the words of the Apostle, "putting away lying, speak every man truth with his neighbour"—that is, with *every* body—for we are *all* neighbours, in the scripture language, and *all* of us "members one of another." Speak the truth at all times, without any mixture of deceit or reserve. If you have committed a fault at any time, don't conceal or deny it; because that is committing a still greater, and adding sin to sin. But own it; acknowledge it; ask pardon for it; and resolve never to do so again. This is the sure way, and the only way, to be forgiven, both by God and man. And I charge you, above all things, never to lay your own fault upon another, who is innocent; for that is a double lie, and a great injury, added to lying. But then take notice, on the other hand, that you must not tell a lie to screen any body that is in fault, or to save him from punishment—for this is a false good-nature; and lying is always a fault, and a sin, whatever may be the end proposed by it. In this, as in every other case, there is one sure rule to go by; we must not "do evil that good may come." We must not endeavour to screen, or serve any body at the expence of truth.

Lastly; every kind of deceit whatsoever, whether by word or action, partakes of the nature and guilt of lying, and will be punished accordingly. As murderers and liars are joined together in scripture, so are bloody and deceitful men. "Thou shalt destroy them that speak leasing" (that is, liars) "the Lord will abhor
the

the bloody and deceitful man," Pfalm v. 6—
and again, lv. 23.—But while thefe, and all
other wicked perfons, " fhall be turned into
hell;" let us remember for our comfort that
whofoever "walketh uprightly," or lives a good
and honeft life, and fpeaketh the truth from his
heart; that backbiteth not with his tongue, nor
doeth evil to his neighbour;" he " fhall abide in
the tabernacle of the Lord, and dwell in his
holy hill," that is, in heaven, for ever and ever.

ADMONITION XX.

Exodus xxiii. 2—former part.
Thou fhalt not follow a multitude to do evil.

BEWARE OF BAD EXAMPLES.—You are now
young; and, I truft, as to any great offences, innocent. But you will foon enter into
a wicked world, where you will meet with a
multitude of evil doers: who, not content with
being wicked themfelves, will endeavour to
draw in others, to be their companions in fin.
They will take advantage of your ignorance and
inexperience; will laugh at you, perhaps, for
being good and virtuous; and ufe all their arts
and perfuafions to make you as bad as themfelves. Therefore, I fay unto you again, BE-
WARE. In your bible you will find many earneft and powerful warnings to this purpofe.
Let me beg of you to give them the attention
they deferve, and to treafure them up in your
minds—" My fon," fays Solomon, " if fin-
D ners

ners entice thee, confent thou not. Enter not into the path of the wicked, and go not in the way of evil men. Avoid it, pafs not by it; turn from it, and pafs away." For " the words of the wicked are to lie in wait for blood;" and their " counfels are deceit." So again, in the New Teftament—" Be not deceived," fays St. Paul: " evil communications corrupt good manners." And St. Peter: " Beware left ye alfo, being led away with the error of the wicked, fall from your own ftedfaftnefs."

To anfwer the gracious end and defign of God in thefe cautions and admonitions, was our firft view and purpofe in fetting up thefe Sunday-fchools. It was to keep you out of bad ways, and from following bad examples; as our next was, to train you up in the right way, in the paths of religion and virtue. And as there is no day when more bad examples are to be found, and more evil going forward than on Sunday; perhaps none, that is fpent fo idly and fhamefully by the wicked; we thought it the firft ftep to be taken to bring you, on that facred day, into this place of inftruction, and to fee you go regularly to church—to fee you " go with the multitude," not of evil-doers, but of fuch as the Pfalmift fpeaks of, who go " to the houfe of God, with the voice of joy and praife," to keep his day holy. So far we have the plea-fure to think we have done our duty, and you your's. But it will fignify little, that you fpend *Sunday* well, unlefs you fpend the whole week well likewife. The good inftructions you receive

ceive on *this* day are defigned to regulate your
conduct *every* day: for every day in the week
has its proper bufinefs and employment belong-
ing to it, as well as Sunday. "Six days fhalt
thou labour and do all thy work"—which it is
as much your duty to do, faithfully and diligently, as it is to keep holy the feventh. And
as you are commanded on all days alike, to do
what is right and good, fo are you forbid to do
what is wrong and evil. The warning, or pro-
hibition, in the text belongs to *every* day; to
every hour and minute of the day. It fhould
never be out of our thoughts. For there is always, and ever will be, a multitude of evil-doers;
and we are always in danger of being led away
by them. You muft therefore be always upon
your guard. "Watch and pray, that ye enter not
into temptation." When you fay the Lord's
prayer, in particular (which I hope you do, feri-
oufly and devoutly, every day of your lives) you
fhould earneftly befeech God to "deliver you
from evil;"—that is, not only from the devil,
who is called the *evil one*, as he is the author and
promoter of all wickednefs; but alfo from evil
men, who are his children and inftruments; that
you may not follow, or be led aftray by, them.
And to your prayers you muft in this, as in every
other cafe, join your own hearty endeavours, and
ufe all your care and watchfulnefs, for the fame
purpofe. Avoid all bad people as much as you
can. If they follow you, turn away: fhun them
as you would a plague or peftilence. "Have
no fellowfhip with the unfruitful works of dark-

nefs;"

nefs;" that is, with the workers of wickednefs. Have no familiarity, no intimacy, with them. If you have, depend on it you will catch their wicked ways, and be ruined. It was a wife and noble refolution of David, that he "would not *know* a wicked perfon." The meaning is, that he would fhew them no countenance or favour; would not fuffer fuch to "dwell within his houfe," or even to "tarry in his fight."—My good children, as you advance in life, you muft expect to meet with many wicked perfons: but when you know them to be fo, have nothing to fay, or to do with them; left you add to the multitude of evil doers. You are warned of your danger betimes. Thank God that you are fo, and make a right ufe of the warning. Believe me, it will be no excufe for you in the day of judgment, to fay that the number of finners was great, and that you did only as others did. Remember, the text is plain and pofitive;—no words can be plainer—"Thou fhalt not follow a multitude to do evil." The *number* of finners can never alter the *nature* of fin, or fcreen the finner from the wrath and punifhment of God. As, on the contrary, the way of holinefs will no lefs furely lead to his favour, and to eternal happinefs, however "few there may be that find it." Be ye therefore followers of them, who through faith, and well doing, fhall "inherit the promifes:" knowing, that whoever you follow in this world, the fame you muft follow in the world to come: either the wicked "into everlafting punifhment;" or "the righteous into life eternal."

ADMONITION XXI.

Hebrews xiii. 16.

To do good, and to communicate, forget not : for with such sacrifices God is well pleased.

Among the Jews, sacrifices made a great part of their religious worship. God Almighty ordained them for wise and good purposes; partly, as a token of their subjection and obligation to Him, as their supreme Lord and law-giver; but (as it is generally supposed) principally, to lead their thoughts, and direct their faith, towards the great sacrifice, that was one day to be offered for all mankind. Since the offering of this all-sufficient sacrifice of Christ on the cross, others have entirely ceased: except only the figurative sacrifice of an holy and good life, which was always, and ever will be, of high value in the sight of God. Even under the law he declared that " obedience was better than sacrifice;" and that he desired " mercy," and the knowledge of God (that is, the *practical* knowledge of him, or obedience to his will) " more than burnt offerings." Under the Gospel, as I said, that is the only sacrifice required: and it is absolutely and indispensably required; both as an evidence of our gratitude to God, and as the condition of our reaping the benefit of the sacrifice of our blessed Redeemer. " I beseech you therefore, brethren," (says St. Paul) " by the mercies of God, that ye present your

bodies

bodies a living facrifice, holy, acceptable unto God, which is your reafonable fervice," and in like manner, in the text; " To do good, and to communicate, forget not : for with fuch facrifices God is well pleafed."

But you will fay perhaps, How does this precept concern *you ?*—how can *you* do good in your *low* ftation of life ? or what have you to fpare to give to *others*, who have fo little of *your own*, and are obliged to work for your daily bread?—I hope to fhew you very plainly, that you have it in your power to do *much* good; and if you have, it certainly is your duty to do it. I hope too to convince you, that you may have opportunities of communicating, or parting with, fomething to others more needy than yourfelves, and when you have, you certainly ought to lay hold on them.

In the firft place, I would have you obferve, that every good perfon, whatever his ftation may be, is an ufeful member of fociety, and therefore does good to it. In the body of Chriftians, as in the natural body, every member, from the higheft to the loweft, has his proper office affigned him; which if he fills, and difcharges the duties of it, as he ought, he in fome fort contributes to the good of the whole. Befides, he does good by his example. It is an old and a true remark, that example is more powerful than precept: fo apt are we to catch the manners of thofe we keep company with. As a wicked man has more to anfwer for than his own fins, by the influence of his bad example

on

on others: so a good one has the pleasure to reflect, that besides his own virtues, he has been the happy instrument of raising, or forwarding, the like good seeds among his neighbours. There is a very strong and beautiful expression to this purpose in the epistle to the Hebrews; where the apostle exhorts them to "*provoke* unto love, and to good works"—that is, to stir up, to excite, to cause a sort of contention and emulation, one with another, in the discharge of kind and good offices.—Thus much in general.

But to be more particular.—You may all of you do good to your parents, and other relations, by working for them, and being of service to them in an hundred different ways, too many to mention in this place. You may, in like manner, do good to your friends and neighbours, in a variety of instances. You may attend the sick; assist the helpless; comfort the afflicted. Children and young people, by their quickness and activity, may often be of great use in helping those that are older; and when they shew a ready disposition to be so, their services are doubly acceptable. The affectionate and dutiful attention of a son, or daughter, cheers the heart of a parent, and in that respect may be said to do him good. Love and kindness to a brother, or sister, or neighbour, is always pleasing, and is often of real benefit. In short, if you are really inclined, and desirous, to do good, you will never want opportunities of doing it. The whole life of our blessed Saviour was so employed. We are told, that he " went

about

about doing good ;" and it is our duty, and should be our constant endeavour, to follow his example.

The other part of the direction in the text is, " not to forget to communicate,"—that is, to remember to give, or impart, to others, somewhat of our own, which they may stand in need of. And this you may all do, more or less, however small your portion may be of this world's goods: for there are few so poor, but others are poorer. Nor will your gift, however slender, be without its value or reward. Remember, how highly the widow's two mites were prized by our Lord, as it was " all that she had;" and therefore she was considered by him as casting in more than all the rich, who contributed only a small portion out of their abundance. And remember what he says upon another occasion: " Whosoever shall give to drink unto one of these little ones, a cup of cold water only, in the name of a disciple ; verily I say unto you, he shall in no wise lose his reward."

ADMONITION XXII.

PSALM xxxix. 1.

*I said, I will take heed to my ways, that I sin
not with my tongue.*

A TRULY wife faying, and pious refolution,
which we ought all of us to follow. " Set
a watch, O Lord, before my mouth: keep the
door of my lips;" was David's prayer, and
fhould be our's. For as " in many things we
offend all;" fo there is none, perhaps, in which
we are fo liable and apt to offend, as in our
fpeech, or with our tongue. The offences of
it are fo various, and the opportunities of committing them fo frequent, that it requires all our
care and circumfpection to guard againft them.
And happy the man who has fo far the command of himfelf as to keep clear of them. For
" if any man offend not in word," fays the
apoftle, " the fame is a perfect man, and able
alfo to bridle the whole body." By the maftery
of his tongue, he fhews that he can fubdue all
his irregular paffions and appetites; and comes
as near as may be to the character of perfection,
or to that of a good and compleat Chriftian.

I fhall point out to you the feveral fins, or
offences of the tongue: and may God give you
grace to avoid them!

The firft, and higheft, of thefe is curfing and
fwearing; a fin of the moft heinous nature, for

D 5 which

which there is not the leaſt ſhadow of excuſe. I really want words to deſcribe the exceſſive wickedneſs of it. It is ſetting the Almighty at defiance; daring his vengeance; and offering him the groſſeſt inſult. It is, beſides, the greateſt breach of charity to our fellow creatures. One would think it the ſin of *devils*, rather than of *men*. The tongue of the ſwearer may be truly ſaid to be " ſet on fire of hell."

Another offence of the mouth againſt God, is the uſing his name careleſsly and inconſiderately in common converſation. This is certainly inconſiſtent with that reſpect, and reverence, which is due to him. Even to ſay, Good God! or Oh Lord! or any ſuch expreſſion, is wrong and diſreſpectful. The ſacred names of God, and of Chriſt, ſhould never be uſed but in prayer, or on ſome very ſolemn occaſion.

The next ſin of the tongue I ſhall mention, is that of ſlandering, or abuſing, our neighbour. And, however common the practice, it is always ſpoken of in ſcripture as a ſin of the deepeſt dye. " Whiſperers, and backbiters;" are placed by St. Paul among the very worſt of ſinners— " haters of God," as well as injurious to men. And in another black catalogue of wicked perſons, he ſays expreſsly, that " revilers" *ſhall not* " inherit the kingdom of God." Slandering, or ſpreading falſe reports of another, is the worſt ſort of that abominable ſin of lying; which having treated of in a diſcourſe by itſelf, I ſhall ſay nothing more of it at preſent: but ſhall rather caution you againſt that kind of evil ſpeaking,

3

which

which tho' perhaps it keeps within the bounds of truth, is still hurtful to our neighbour, and therefore condemned in scripture, as a breach of our duty to him. Under this head is included all uncharitable and censorious discourse—whatever tends to hurt another's reputation, or to give him uneasiness. Accordingly, St. Paul charges Titus to admonish his disciples, " to speak evil of no man"—and again : " to be no brawlers"—that is, to use no angry, or quarrelsome, language—which is another offence of the tongue ; contrary to all the rules of good manners ; destructive of peace, and good neighbourhood ; and directly opposite to the spirit, and precepts, of our holy religion ; which requires us to be "gentle, meek, and courteous." And here let me particularly warn you against all rude and disrespectful language to your superiors ; especially to your parents, and to your masters and mistresses. They are intitled not barely to civility, but to your dutiful submission, and respect. I charge you never to give them a pert or saucy answer ; never to shew any resentment at what they say to you, but to receive their orders, and take their reproofs, silently and quietly, as becomes good children and servants: always remembering, that if you offend against your parents, or masters, *on earth,* you offend at the same time against your father, and master, who is *in heaven.*

Another sin of the tongue is lewd or indecent discourse ; what the apostle calls " filthy communication." Let no such ever come out of

your

your mouth: and if others use it, turn away from them; for they are most dangerous companions. It is a very great sin, and of the worst consequence; proceeding from a corrupt and wicked heart, and leading to every thing that is shameful and abominable: to what " ought not to be named," much less practised, among Christians.

The last offence I shall mention is that of vain, idle, or foolish talking; which, we are told, is "not convenient," that is, unbecoming, unsuitable to the character of a Christian. It is certainly a less fault than the others I have mentioned. But then observe, that, as little faults lead to great ones, so much foolish discourse generally ends in what is wicked and criminal. It is, at best, a great waste of time, and hindrance of business: according to a vulgar but true saying, that great *talkers* are little *doers*. And Solomon tells us, " that in the multitude of words there wanteth not sin." But what I wish you chiefly to attend to, and often seriously to think of, is that awful declaration of our blessed Saviour, with which I shall conclude. " I say unto you, that every *idle* word that men speak, they shall give account thereof in the day of judgment—For by thy words thou shalt be justified; and by thy words thou shalt be condemned."

ADMONITION XXIII.

PSALM cxix. 6.

Then shall I not be ashamed, when I have respect unto all thy commandments.

SHAME is the natural consequence of sin. So it was with our first parents. While they were innocent, we read that they " were not ashamed;" but no sooner had they disobeyed the divine command, than shame and confusion followed. They were " afraid," and hid themselves. Now shame is always accompanied with pain and uneasiness. And it is wisely so ordered by our good and gracious Creator, in order to keep us from sinning: that as we all wish to avoid pain, we should avoid shame which is the cause of it; and refrain from sin, as it is the cause of shame. Do you then desire *not* to be ashamed? Follow the advice of the holy Psalmist Do your duty—obey God in all things— and " then," you may say in the words of the text, " I shall not be ashamed, when I have respect unto all thy commandments."

My first advice to you therefore is " that ye sin not"—that you do nothing to be ashamed of: for there is nothing we ought to be ashamed of but sin. However, since, notwithstanding all your care and endeavours, you will sometimes fail in your duty; my next advice is, that whenever

ever you do offend, you take shame to yourselves for so doing. For shame leads to sorrow,
and sorrow (if it be sincere) to amendment.
There is a *godly* shame, as well as " a godly sorrow" (as the apostle calls it), which " worketh
repentance." Be ashamed therefore of having
done wrong; but never be ashamed of owning
it. If you confess your faults, with shame and
concern, and with a firm resolution of never
committing the like again, they will be forgiven
you. To be without shame, or without feeling,
for one's sins, is a sure sign of a most depraved and hardened heart. One part of St.
Paul's description of the most abandoned men
is, that they glory " in their shame,"—or boast
of those sins which they ought to be ashamed
of.

But there is a false and bad shame, too common among all, and especially among young
people, which I must caution you against, as being destructive of all virtue and goodness. I
mean, a shame of doing one's duty. Hear what
our Saviour says of it : " Whosoever shall be
ashamed of me, and of my words, of him shall
the Son of Man be ashamed, when he shall
come" to judgment. Think only, what it is, to
be ashamed of Christ, and to have Christ
ashamed of you. Surely you must be shocked
at the thought of it, and tremble at the consequence: to hear him say, at that awful day, " I
know you not—depart from me."—Now to be
ashamed of the " words" of Christ, is to be
ashamed of living according to the laws and

rules of his gospel: and this is, in fact, being ashamed of Christ himself. It is disowning him for our Lord and Master. For it signifies nothing to acknowledge him with our *mouths*, if we deny him by our *actions*. "If a man love me," says he, "he will keep my words:" which no one can do, who is ashamed of them. This false shame is like that false fear, which is condemned and forbidden in scripture, as inconsistent with a religious and good life. "The fear of man," says Solomon, "bringeth a snare." And God himself says, by the prophet Isaiah, "Fear ye not the reproach of men, neither be ye afraid of their revilings." In both places are meant bad and wicked men, who will laugh at the good and upright for their virtue and godliness, and try by their infamous ridicule, and reproaches, to make them as bad as themselves. But never, I charge you, be afraid of them, or of their revilings. Never be ashamed of serving God, and doing your duty. Good men will love and esteem you for it, and God will reward you. "Them that honour him," he has declared that "he will honour." Though you may be despised and scoffed at on earth by the wicked and profane, you will be honoured in heaven before men and angels, and receive "a crown of glory that fadeth not away." This world is a state of trial; and bad men are a trial to the good. They are a snare to us in many respects; but in none perhaps more, than by endeavouring to give a wrong turn to those principles of shame and fear, which our Maker has

implanted

implanted in us for the wiseft and beft purpofes. A fenfe of fhame was defigned to keep us from fin; or, if we have finned, to lead us to repent-ance. The fear of God was intended to keep us from offending him; to make us " hate evil," and " have refpect unto all his com-mandments." Quite contrary to thefe are the falfe fhame and fear, which the wicked wifh, and' endeavour, to inftil into us: a fhame of doing our duty, and a fear of being laughed at for it. But we may reft affured, for our com-fort, that God, who fuffers us to be thus tried, will carry us fafe through the trial, if we pray to him for his grace and affiftance, and join thereto our own hearty endeavours. He has warned us of our danger, and fhown us how to efcape it. While we truft in his power and goodnefs, and do our beft to ferve him in all holy and godly living, we have nothing to fear, and can have nothing to be afhamed of. Let us therefore, after the example of St. Paul, approve our-felves in all things as the faithful Servants of God; " by honour, and difhonour; by evil re-port, and good report."—little folicitous about the treatment we meet with in *this* world; but " looking," with faith and patience, " for the coming of our Lord Jefus Chrift," who fhall " reward every man according to his works."

ADMONITION XXIV.

To the PARENTS.

EPHESIANS vi. 4.

—— *Bring them up in the nurture and admonition of the Lord.*

THE great usefulness and necessity of a virtuous and religious education (which the apostle here enforces) are so very apparent, that I should hope it were needless to say any thing to you in proof or confirmation of it. But the misfortune is, that the plainest truths, though ever so important, are often overlooked and disregarded; perhaps merely because they are plain. Let me however intreat you to consider, seriously and frequently, how much it is both your duty and interest, to bring up your children in the ways of godliness, virtue, and industry; and how much your own happiness, as well as their's, in this life, as well as in the next, will depend upon it. You seem indeed to be sensible of this, by sending your children to partake of the instructions of our school: and so far you do well. But alas! all we can do for them will signify little, unless you join your endeavours to our's to " train them up," and keep them, " in the way wherein they should go ;" and above all, unless you confirm by *your example* what they learn from *our precepts.* Children will

4   imitate

imitate their parents; and if they see at *home* a practice and behaviour quite contrary to what they are taught at *school*, our labour will be lost, and our best advice thrown away upon them. For their sakes, therefore, as well as for your own, let me beg of you to be particularly circumspect both in your words and actions: to refrain from every vicious and bad course, and to be patterns of whatever is good and praiseworthy. Watch carefully over their behaviour, and when you see any thing wrong, check it immediately, that it may not grow into a bad habit. If at any time you observe a disposition to lying, deceit, or thieving, reprove them sharply; and if words will not do, you must have recourse to the rod. But for lesser faults, and carelessness, a gentle and mild reproof is to be preferred. Hear them sometimes read; and try, if possible, to make them remember what they read. Hear them say their prayers; and take care that they say them slowly, deliberately, and devoutly: the Lord's prayer particularly so, (*See* Admonition VII.) And do not forget, I intreat you, to add your own prayers to their's, and to our's, that it would please God to prosper the work we are engaged in; to make your children good and useful members of society; a blessing and comfort to their parents and friends.

ADMONITION XXV.

To the PARENTS and others.

1 COR. v. 8.

Let us keep the feaſt.

IT is much to be lamented, that the feſtivals of the church, which were deſigned to anſwer the beſt purpoſes, are, by a ſad perverſion of them, made to ſerve the worſt. Of theſe there is none perhaps ſo groſsly abuſed, or ſo ſcandalouſly profaned, as that of Chriſtmas. A ſeaſon wiſely ſet apart for the commemoration of our bleſſed Lord's coming into the world, to " *deſtroy* the works of the Devil," is by too many made the occaſion of *promoting* them : and CHRIST, the great pattern and preacher of holineſs, is thereby made " the miniſter of ſin." What are commonly called (and would properly be ſo called, if rightly obſerved) the Chriſtmas *holy* days, become, by this ſhameful abuſe of them, the moſt *unholy* of all the days in the year: being ſpent in ſloth and idleneſs, in rioting and drunkenneſs, and in all manner of vice and debauchery. When we are called upon more particularly to remember our Saviour, and his exceeding great love and mercy towards us, we ſeem moſt of all to forget him, and to forfeit all pretenſions to his favour. When (as the apoſtle directs, and as our church

teaches

teaches us to pray) we should "*put off* the works of darknefs," or fin, we *run into them* " with greedinefs:" and when we ought, with peculiar care and zeal, to " put *on* the Lord Jefus Chrift," (that is, to adorn ourfelves with every Chriftian grace and virtue) we may be faid to put him off, and by our conduct to renounce our holy profeffion. Inftead of obferving a *Chriftian* feftival, we feem to copy after the *heathenifh* rites of the antient Romans; who held a feaft at the latter end of December, in which they were allowed to commit all forts of excefs and licentioufnefs. They indeed had ignorance to plead, and in fome fenfe acted in character, as being followers of falfe gods, who were in fact the inftruments of Satan, and confequently the patrons of fin. But we, who worfhip the true God, know better, and are therefore without excufe. We know that by every fin we commit, we "blafpheme that worthy," and holy, " name by which we are called." Better, I am fure, far better it would be, that there were no holydays at all, than that they fhould be kept in fuch a manner as they are. Better to *forget* the birth of Chrift altogether, than to *pretend* to *remember* it, and at the fame time to act in direct oppofition to the end and defign of it. St. Paul, warning the Ephefians againft the diforderly and vicious people of his days, fays, " it is a fhame even to fpeak of thofe things which are done of them *in fecret*." Surely it is a great fhame to fee and hear the things which are done and fpoken by the rioters of our time *openly*, and in

public;

public ; and this at a feafon fet apart for the ex-
ercife of religion and good works. It is fhock-
ing—it is fcandalous——But let *us*, my brethren, " keep the feaft" (every feftival of our
church in general, and this moft facred one of
Chriftmas in particular) in a manner fuitable to
its nature and folemnity. Let us keep it, as the
apoftle directs, in " fincerity and truth," that is,
as an holy and religious feaft. Befides attending the public offices of the church, let us meditate in private on the great and undeferved
bleffings as at this time derived from heaven,
and confider how we may make a right ufe of
them, and a proper return for them. Let us
employ our time, and our thoughts (a more delightful employment there cannot be) in con-
templating the love of God in fending his only-
begotten Son into the world, to live, and to die,
for us : and the love of Chrift in coming, and
giving himfelf a ranfom and facrifice for us.
Let us filently admire and adore, as well as ce-
lebrate in the congregation of the faithful, the
exceeding riches and wonders of his love and
goodnefs towards us. And let it be our peculiar ftudy at *this* time, as it fhould be our conftant endeavour at *all* times, to live as becomes
the redeemed of the Lord. Kind and good
offices to one another, *always* indeed feafonable,
are *now* more particularly fo. " If God fo
loved us, we ought alfo to love one another ;"
and to fhew our love by our actions. Our dear
Redeemer, during his abode on earth, " went
about

about doing good." Let us follow his example, while we commemorate his birth.

But, you may fay perhaps, "are our holydays to be paffed wholly in acts of piety and charity?" Certainly not. Some time may, and ought to, be allowed for the focial meeting, the cheerful meal, and friendly converfation. Chriftmas is juftly accounted a joyful feafon, and ought to be kept as fuch. " Let the righteous" (*now* more efpecially) " be glad and rejoice before God: let them alfo be merry and joyful." And, believe me, none but the righteous can be truly fo.——To conclude: Do your duty to God and men; enjoy the company of your friends and neighbours; eat and drink with ftrict temperance and fobriety; and then you will not fail to have, what I heartily wifh you, A COMFORTABLE AND AN HAPPY CHRISTMAS.

F I N I S.

Lately Published,

FOR J. WALTER, AT HOMER'S HEAD, CHARING-CROSS;
AND F. AND C. RIVINGTON, ST. PAUL'S CHURCH-
YARD.

I. AN ESSAY on the HOLY SACRAMENT of the LORD's SUPPER, addreffed to the Inhabitants of a populous Parifh near London. By PETER WALDO, Efq; of Mitcham, in Surry. Price 1 *s.*

†‡† The Society for promoting Chriftian Knowledge have added this Effay on the Sacrament to their Lift of Books made ufe of and recommended by the Society. And, a Clergyman in the Neighbourhood of London fo fully approved the Effay, that, with Permiffion of the Author, he has printed large Impreffions at his own private Expence, to diftribute among his Parifhioners and Friends.

II. A COMMENTARY, PRACTICAL and EXPLANATORY, on the LITURGY of the CHURCH of ENGLAND, as ufed on SUNDAYS: Including the Athanafian Creed. By the Author of the above Effay on the Sacrament. In one Volume 8vo. Price 5 *s.* bound.

Let every man ftudy his Prayers, and read his Duty in his Petitions.
                                        BISHOP TAYLOR.

www.ingramcontent.com/pod-product-compliance
Lightning Source LLC
Chambersburg PA
CBHW081517040426
42447CB00013B/3256